Qr...

The Almighty You

Your apprehension. It

earnest desire to take your 4

and ease your hurts.

What has happened in your

life was ordered by the Father. Seek

Solice in knowing you have found

favor with God.

Today you understand not,

but rest assured in the days

ahead, you will see, and realize

His intentions. Qr. seek God, He will

reveal Himself to those who

earnestly seek Him.

Brenda L Boyd

Soul'D Out

Brenda L. Boyd

authorHOUSE®

AuthorHouse™
1663 Liberty Drive
Bloomington, IN 47403
www.authorhouse.com
Phone: 1-800-839-8640

First published by AuthorHouse 10/16/2009

ISBN: 978-1-4490-3358-3 (e)
ISBN: 978-1-4490-3356-9 (sc)
ISBN: 978-1-4490-3357-6 (hc)

Printed in the United States of America
Bloomington, Indiana

This book is printed on acid-free paper.

Contents

Acknowledgments

I want to take this opportunity to thank my family, who believed in me when the odds were stacked against me. My parents, who selected each other, created us (together with God) and stayed united despite the obstacles. You raised your children in the way you should, allowing us to spread our wings and affording each of us the opportunity to fly.

To my three children, without whom my life would serve no purpose! When God looked at me and saw that my life was incomplete, He blessed me with the three of you. I realize that you are truly God's gift to me, and for that alone I am eternally grateful. Thank you for assisting me in my endeavor to achieve, but mostly for loving me unconditionally in spite of life's obstacles. I could not be more proud of the three of you, and I credit God with each milestone you attain. Keep reaching, my beloved children, for nothing is out of your grasp as long as God is your leader.

To all the youth who have ever allowed me the privilege of being a mentor to them, my ability to do so stems from my desire to watch you grow in Christ. It was each of you who inspired me to keep the course, and I truly thank you. Keep the faith, my children, when life's path seems too hard to walk upon. Always remember it is then that your Heavenly Father is carrying you. On a personal note, I have always looked at each of you as individuals, judged you not, and loved you unconditionally. Thank you for loving me in the same manner.

Above all I want to thank the God of all the universe, who picked up clay, formed it, breathed life into it, and created me in His image. Without you, Heavenly Father, this book would have no reason or purpose. Because of you and you alone, I am able to write this. God, I pray obstacles be removed from the lives of those who are about to enter into a realm of love so great that not even the human mind can comprehend. Help me to reveal to those you love that you are totally *Soul'D Out* in love with each person who has ever believed their life has no meaning.

Introduction
All odds against you

Feeling as though everything in life that can go wrong already has and believing that nothing else will transpire. But then here I go again picking up the pieces of another disaster only to find there is another hidden behind the door called life. If I am the apple of His eye, why must I go through this again? If He loves me beyond all measure, why is this happening to me? I can't meet my bills; my husband left; the kids expect more and more of me; and the world is asking me to believe in products that will renew, clothes that will express, crèmes that will rejuvenate, and sex appeal that will bring unspeakable joy at any age. People, the media will dress you, advertisements will subject you to the newest items of pleasure, but when the obstacles of life are stacked against you, there is only One who can satisfy the emptiness that dwells deep within your soul.

Whom do I want to read this? Anyone who has ever faced obstacles that seem so overwhelming they don't know how they will pick up the pieces of a seemingly broken life and start over. All those who ever covered themselves in cardboard to keep the night's chill from stealing their warmth. Those who enter the world of the unknown to keep from feeling the rejection of life's trials. Those who drank themselves into oblivion searching for answers in the emptiness of a bottle only to find that at the bottom was nothing more than a circle of colored glass. Every prostitute who ever had to sell himself or herself to make ends meet, feed a family, or supply a habit.

I am about to dig so deep inside of you that you are going to think I have a camera hidden deep within your mind and am able to read your very thoughts. There is an answer to your obstacles no matter how big or how small they are. That answer resides with the One, who is *Soul'D Out* in love with you. Not you, you say? Hold on my friend. I wrote this on behalf of Him with you in mind!

Obstacles

"We have to talk! I've been doing some thinking. There's no easy way to say this, so I will just come out and say it. I'm leaving! I've had enough, and I can't take it anymore. I'm leaving, and I'm taking the kids with me! There's nothing you can do or say that will change my mind. I'm just not happy anymore. It's for the best you'll see."

"Yes sir! They said you wanted to see me."

"Take a seat. You know that over the past year things have been a lot slower than years past. Word came from the top this morning that we must downsize. I'm sorry but your last day is the end of this month."

"But, but my wife—she's pregnant—and what about our new house?"

"I'm sorry, there's nothing I can do; it's beyond my control, but don't worry, it'll all work out. You'll see."

"Hi doc, you said you have something to show me!"

"Yes, your tests have come back, and they don't look good. There are several spots on your lungs. All tests indicate that you have cancer."

"How much time, Doc?"

"I give you maybe two months. I would suggest that you get all your affairs in order. I know this comes as a shock to you, but there's absolutely nothing else we can do. We will make you as comfortable as we can; you'll see."

"Who could be calling at this hour?"

"Ma'am, this is the highway patrol. Your son has been in an accident. We are on—"

"Is he all right? My son, is he all right?"

"I'm sorry, ma'am, we did all we could do. Could someone please come? We have your son's personal items, and we want to make sure you get them. I'm real sorry about this, ma'am. It will take time but eventually you'll be okay; you'll see."

"I hate you. I hate you both. You're the meanest parents a kid could ever have. All I want to do is go and spend some time with my friends, but no. You think you know them, but you really don't. I swear I can't wait to turn eighteen so I can move out. I'll show you, I will never come back. You'll see!"

"Obstacle," defined by *Webster*, is a barrier, hindrance, interruption, or obstruction. It disrupts your normal life, becoming an object of distraction, causing you to doubt yourself, interfering with your family, and at times leading you to believe that you are slowly losing ground on this walk called life. Often times you feel you are losing touch with reality. Sad to say, you may believe you are alone. But hold on my friend; you are not alone. You are not the only one who ever faced an obstacle so large that running away seemed to be the only way.

About three years ago a group of youth chaperones and I went on a mission trip; our goal was to minister to the homeless. We spent endless weeks of studying, preparing, and praying for God's will for this trip. But nothing really could have prepared us for what we were about to see. We arrived at the shelter, were briefed, and asked what we had expected to learn from this trip. I personally had one goal in mind—to meet the woman God had laid on my heart. He told me there would be a prostitute that would come, and my only goal was to tell her that He loved her. I should not leave her until she understood that He didn't care what she did yesterday, today, or tomorrow. He loved her unconditionally. He said, "If I go up to the heavens, you are there; if I make my bed in the depths, you are there." (Ps. 139:8 NIV)

The days that followed were busy: supplying cloths to those in need, ministering to the children of those to whom God had called His own. Later that evening a major turning point happened for all of us. We visited a beautiful park in the area, getting there before dark and leaving as the sun went down to avoid the dangers that lay ahead. Loading back into the buses, we toured the inner city streets that many of the homeless called home. It was there that all the thoughts that had ever crossed my mind about people being homeless by their own choices or their own doing slowly vanished. Obstacles had put some of them where they were. Our guide told us a story that forever changed my attitude toward those whose obstacle diminished their desire to live because their burden was more than they could bear. My friend, God sent His son for you and me to live our lives to their fullest: "The thief comes only to steal and kill and destroy; I have come that they may have life and have it to the full." (John 10:10 NIV)

Everyone wants to be on top, but what happens when all of a sudden you fall off the top and reach rock bottom? What happens when you have everything and without warning it's gone? My perception of homelessness changed when our guide shared the following story with us. A doctor climbing the ladder of success had it all: a recent promotion, a beautiful wife, three kids, everything one man could ask for. Until tragedy hit and his life was forever changed. The doctor decided to go out and celebrate his recent promotion, but he neglected to call his wife and inform her of this decision. Hours later, his wife began to worry about his whereabouts. Unable to reach him, the doctor's wife loaded their three children in the car and began the journey to her husband's place of employment to see if perhaps his car had broken down. While she searched for her missing husband, her car was broadsided by a drunk driver, killing the precious cargo inside—the three children and her.

This obstacle was too great for one man to handle, no matter how successful he might have been. The doctor lost everything—giving up his house, his promotion, his dignity—because he could not live his life with the thought of his family's deaths forever haunting him. On his arm, he wore a delicate picture of a vine cascading upward. The vine contained four roses, one for each of those he lost that unforgettable day. Unfortunately, when this once successful doctor looked at this beautiful piece of art, all he saw was a vine with four skulls on it. Death stole his reason for living, for going on. He began looking for the answers to his obstacle at the bottom of a bottle, all the while keeping the nights air off of him by covering himself with a box. He lost all desire to ever pick up the pieces and start again. How about you, my friend? Where are you looking for the answers to the obstacle that's found its way into your life?

I found the prostitute that God had laid on my heart months earlier. In confidence she shared with me that she had not bathed in three days. With a tear glistening in the corner of her eye, she told me she had two older children she had not seen in quite some time. Leaning forward, I reached for her, fulfilling that which God had asked me to do. I put my arms around her, and she began to weep uncontrollably as I told her that God loved her just as she was. Time seemed to stand still as she continued to cry, and tears ran down this once beautiful face, now aged from years of street living. Finally she released her grip, looked at me, and thanked me for the words that brought peace to her heart. If this is you, my beautiful lady, reading this book, His love for you still abounds. He is *Soul'D Out* in love with you, I promise.

As I laid my head down that night, many thoughts went through my mind, none as dear as the smile that covered my dear lady's face when she knew she was truly loved. My heart could not even fathom what obstacles had brought those among us to where they were, but I realized that no matter how great the obstacle that so often sets us back, there is One who understands, comprehends, and has also traveled down this same road before us. My friend, He wants you to know that He has already overcome these obstacles that constantly hold us bound: "I have told you these things, so that in me you may have peace. In this world you will have trouble. But take heart! I have overcome the world." (John 16:33 NIV)

I am about to share a story with you about an obstacle so large that the only way to overcome it was to go through it. It's a story so often told that we just seem to let it enter our mind and exit as quickly as it entered. It's the story of a man born to save the world from definite disaster. He made the ultimate sacrifice for every man, woman, and child. This, my friend, includes you! Hold on, your obstacle is about to be overcome by the One who overcame each of life's obstacles with you in mind. You'll see!

Status Quo

Ever hear a story about a hero? There were countless numbers of heroic stories told in the days and weeks that followed the tragedy of 9/11, stories that brought tears to many of us who watched the days unfold before our eyes. There were the stories about the firemen who ran into burning buildings to rescue people they never new, not hesitating a moment to take into account that they might never make it out alive. Police officers risked it all and entered buildings that they would never make it out of, yet along the way they helped someone else to safety. They forgot about their own lives to save others. Some say, "That's their job; they took an oath." Others believe that they were coerced to enter the burning buildings by their superiors. I personally believe that they did what they did because their life meant nothing unless they sacrificed it all.

We can read stories about heroes in books of all forms. Movies are made about them, and television thrives on documentaries of people who went above and beyond. Heroes come in all shapes, sizes, and colors. You may even know one, someone who has done the unthinkable, exquisitely showing bravery above the call of duty. Medals are placed on the chests of many of our finest heroes for defending the "land of the free and the home of the brave." Monuments have been erected to remember fallen heroes as an act of gratitude for a job well done and in recognition of the sacrifices they made. There are walls all around the world inscribed with the names of thousands of fallen heroes who died for a cause, a belief, a freedom, or a battle won.

What about the unsung heroes, the individuals who never receive recognition for their act of bravery? Their actions are overlooked, thought to be trivial, or seemed so ordinary that they weren't worth recognizing: the mother left behind in the face of a tragedy to raise children on her own, in a world set on disrupting anything that resembles a family; the school principal who has to pick up the pieces after a school shooting and face hundreds of angry faces unsure that he did everything he could to prevent such an evil act of violence; the widow terrified to go out at night because of the evils that lurk around every corner; the nurse who stopped to help, but all she could do was comfort as the last breath of life drained from the individual she held. How about you, ever do anything heroic in your life? Sometimes the simplest things in life can be the greatest act of heroism in the life of someone else.

Jesus Christ was himself a hero of astronomical proportions. He went beyond that which could be expected from any one being. However, He has received more criticism and caused more controversy than most people. Theologians try to dispel the fact that he ever existed, and for some unknown reason, the human race seems to remember Him only when the need arises. No one before Him or after Him has rightfully earned a hero's status equivalent to His, yet His only rewards were a forsaken kiss from a friend that would forever change His fate, a couple of nails, a wooden cross, an angry mob, and enough criticism to last until the end of time. "But Jesus said to him, 'Judas, are you betraying the Son of Man with a kiss?'" (Luke 22:48 New American Standard)

Jesus didn't come to be anyone's hero. He came to take away your obstacle, your doubts, and your reasons for giving up on life. Let's be honest, I really don't know what Jesus prayed that unforgettable night in the garden, before He was to change the world with one of the greatest acts of bravery ever known to man. But I do know that there was an obstacle of astronomical proportions before him, and He had every reason to run. Fear alone would have caused many of us to run, but not Him. See, He knew His time had come to fulfill His Father's plan for each and every one of us, and He already knew that without Him our destiny would end. Settling for the obstacle in front of Him was not an option. Suffering great anxiety over what awaited him would not and could not contain Him. Do I think that Jesus was in pain that night in the garden? Not physical as one would expect, but I believe He was mentally fighting a battle inside Himself. I often wonder if we knew the suffering He would have to endure whether we would continue on as He did or whether we would run to avoid those obstacles that may set us free. He never quit. He might have felt anguish that night, but there was a battle to be

11

fought, and that battle began even before the kiss that eventually led to Jesus' demise and death: "And being in anguish, he prayed more earnestly, and his sweat was like drops of blood falling on the ground. (Luke 22:44 NIV)

Paul S. Taylor of Eden Communications explains the process of sweating blood, according to Dr. Frederic Zugive, a chief medical examiner. Permit me to help you have a better understanding of our Lords determination to stop at nothing to save the world, despite the obstacle. The clinical term for sweating blood is "hematohidrosis." Around the sweat glands, there are multiple blood vessels. Under pressure, the vessels constrict. As anxiety passes, the blood vessels dilate to the point of rupture. As the sweat glands produce sweat, they push blood to the surface, which causes drops of blood to mix with sweat. My only desire here is for you to fully comprehend that it was the love that Jesus Christ had for each of us that empowered Him to overcome the obstacle. He asked His Father if it was His will to take this obstacle away from Him. He surrendered everything to the mercy of His Father so that you and I could understand what unconditional love truly is. It's a love that knows only mercy and grace, and it was granted to each of us by our Heavenly Father through His beloved Son: "Father, if you are willing, take this cup from me yet not my will, but yours be done." (Luke 22:42 NIV)

Can you fathom it? Not even our largest obstacle would have stopped Him from fulfilling His promise of setting us free? What reason do you have today for not releasing your obstacle to Him?

Jesus has already given all and on your behalf. He already knew what you were going to have to endure. He already knew you would spend endless hours wondering why. He already knew you would shed enough tears to fill an alabaster vessel. That very night in the garden, Jesus surrendered His life for all those who are lost, all those who are hurting, all those who need to overcome the odds, and all those who need to know they're loved more than anything that life has to offer. "For God so loved the world He sent His only begotten son, that whoever believes in Him should not perish, but have eternal life." (John 3:16 NIV) If God sent His son, for you to live life fully, why then are you allowing something or someone to drain you from that which God has promised you?

Just as I am telling you, God told His son. Your battle has been won; victory is yours. Reach up and take hold! The One who fought the good fight might have died that day on Calvary, but He rose to take the victory despite an endless attempt at keeping Him captive. Are you being held captive today by an obstacle that you're running away from instead of running through it? Stop running. The only way you can overcome the obstacle is to go through it. So take a deep breath, stop analyzing the situation, stop contemplating the consequences, and rise up. It's time you roll over your stone and take back what life has been draining from you. Want to do something heroic with your life? Live life as Christ intended you to. I can write the book, tell you how and what to do, but only you can rise up and take back what rightfully belongs to you. What are you waiting for?

Even on His cross—hung as if to humiliate—it was not written that a hero resided there. Jesus became a part of the status quo just by doing His job, not unlike the people mentioned above. We tend to over look the fact that this unsung hero went to His death so that you and I could live life to its fullest not to set the world into a controversial frenzy about His actions. Today is a good day to start living life as it was intended for you to live, no matter what circumstances may have come your way.

The number one excuse for not overcoming battles in our lives is, "You just don't understand. I can't." Maybe I don't understand, but I know someone who does. "How am I supposed to go on when life is closing in all around me?" Ever thought about asking for help? Friends are great, family is even better, but what about the One who holds your future in His hands. To some He might be just a part of the status quo, but let me reassure you, He has the ability to change your situation for the better. Stop looking at Him like He's a hero who had to act the way He did. Instead, look at Him like He's the hero who acted with you on His mind, your name on the palm of His hand, and every hair on the top of your head numbered: "And even the very hairs of your head are all numbered." (Matt. 10:30 NIV)

Maybe He's not the hero with the medal on His chest or among the list of names that hang on walls all over the world, but rest assured He is far greater than the status quo or someone who acted because he had to. Any one person who has caused as much controversy as Jesus Christ did before and after death has to have some sort of advantage over the odds. Even a large stone rolled over the entranceway of His tomb couldn't keep Him bound. A world set against Him couldn't stop Him, a cross couldn't destroy Him, and a tomb couldn't contain Him. Do you think your obstacle is too big for Him to handle? If you're tired of going to bed and getting up the same way every day, why don't you let the One who sacrificed everything take over your situation, set you free, and help you to live the life intended just for you?

He placed the stars in perfect harmony, aligned the planets in perfect orbit, and produced you in His image. Don't you get it? Jesus had every reason to run, but He didn't. He had every reason to quit. He didn't. He had every reason to say no. He didn't. So why are you? Don't allow His sacrifice to be in vain. Claim your victory today. You've hesitated long enough!

The Photograph

My parents recently discovered the world of photography and have become fascinated by the latest techniques, lighting, and equipment used to stop time forever. On a recent photo shoot with my mother, she illustrated how lighting changes shadows, how obstacles can be extracted from a photo, and how you can add something into a photo that wasn't there before to give it more grace or glamour. My father, a photographer as well, takes photos second by second. This technique is known as continuous shooting or rapid fire. Good examples of this method are the photos of a space shuttle on lift off. The photographer continuously shoots until the shuttle is lost in outer space, capturing moments on film in a split second, never missing an instant in time. It's truly fascinating to watch photos unfold before your eyes, creating memories frame-by-frame, never hesitating to capture a moment of uniqueness one click at a time.

Wanting to have a better understanding of photography and the intricate details correlated with it, my mother recommended and scheduled a photo shoot for us. Dressed in her princess-like prom dress, my daughter was on her way to be photographed at several locations with different settings: the ocean with ships sailing behind her, fountains flowing in front of her, flowers about to bloom all around her. These scenes added a touch of elegance to the decor of her photo session. With at least one hundred shots taken, my mom was now ready to critique the photos, editing them to perfection. Touching up the photos, cropping those things that didn't need to be there, transposing trees where garbage cans once rested, she removed all those obstacles that made my daughter look anything less than perfect. Mom with her professional knack of perfecting photographs took what was once a simplistic photo and turned it into a creative piece of art, allowing the photo to come to life before the eyes of the beholder.

I find it amazing what techniques are available to create a photo that makes us look better—our teeth whiter, our skin clearer, years removed from our appearance. With today's technology, there are no limitations as to what we can accomplish in documenting the unforgettable moments in our lives. We want our memories forever captured, frozen on paper, fixed to perfection so that we can tell the stories of our past.

Wouldn't life be great if all we ever had to do was erase the things that didn't look right, that didn't feel good, that hurt incredibly, that set us back, that made us cry, or that took away our desire to exist? Perhaps if we could just add a little of this or crop out a little of that, maybe our lives to could be perfected like our most recent photos. Unfortunately life is not perfect. It's filled with some unpleasant memories, those that we wish we could forget. They seem to find away to implant themselves in our minds and become a constant reminder of days gone by.

The key phrase in the above sentence is "days gone by." Why are some of us constantly looking back on our lives instead of looking ahead to our future? Some of us base our entire future on past experiences, good or bad. Some of us view our future as bleak because that's the way our past has been. I am here to tell you that you can't change yesterday, but you sure can do something about tomorrow. Maybe you're one of the people holding on to past hurts, past letdowns, and past experiences in general. Maybe you think you have life all figured out because you see the way it used to be and think it's way it will always be. I have to tell you something: you're dead wrong! "Jesus replied, 'No one who puts his hand to the plow and looks back is fit for service in the kingdom of God.'" (Luke 9:62 NIV)

Sure life comes with its fair share of ups and downs, and I fully believe some of us receive more than their fair share of downs. This does not require us to examine our whole life in light of them. How are you and I ever going to overcome obstacles in our lives if we can't get past them? If there is one thing I've learned in my life, it is that I can do nothing to change those things that have occurred in the past. I can, however, examine them, look closely at alternatives that could have changed the outcome of my circumstances, and apply that knowledge to the situations currently at hand. Doing so helps me learn from the experience instead of living the rest of my life as a result of the experience.

As a parent, I found it totally amazing when I tried to teach my children—two of whom are now grown—how to do new things. When I taught them to ride a bike, I held the seat, ran beside them, and then let go. They would ride as expected for a while. But as soon as they knew I let go, they fell. My job was to pick them back up, place them back on their bike, and help them start over again. Wanting nothing more than to have them forget that they just fell and got hurt, I encouraged them to get up and try again. I am sure if you're a parent you have done no different then I did, always trying to pick up the pieces of their little lives and encouraging them to get up and continue trying. Isn't it funny, though, that we seem to forget that rule of thumb when we look at our own problems?

As adults, we let past experiences play over again and again like a rewound tape, losing sight of every lesson we ever learned or have taught others. I visualize in my mind God the Father sitting up above in the heavens as He watches us contemplate those things that hold us back or keep us bound. He gently reaches down from the heavens with His loving hands and stands us up and dusts us off. He tries to usher us through past experiences, yet we choose to hold steadfast to our past in our present circumstances, rather than learning from them. God the Father has commanded us to be strong; He said, "For the Lord your God is with you wherever you go." Go means to move on, to keep going. Why then do we come to a complete standstill and let the past have its hold over our future? "Have I not commanded you? Be strong and courageous! Do not tremble or be dismayed, for the

Lord your God is with you wherever you go." (Josh. 1:9 New American Standard)

When developing a roll of film, you receive negatives along with the photos. These negatives allow you the luxury to select which photos you like and don't like and duplicate only the ones that appeal to you. That same procedure is true of digital cameras: you have the ability to select which photos you like from the disc and discard those that do not meet with your approval. That is the standard by which you should live your life. You have the ability to keep the negatives in your life, duplicate them repeatedly, or get rid of them. Don't you think it's time the past stays just that? Isn't it time to start integrating those things that aren't negative into your life?

My daughter is famous for saying, "Mom you never know. This could be a photo opportunity." The unexpected could happen right before our eyes, and we should be prepared. Just like her or any other photographer, you have to be looking for the unexpected. If you are not prepared when the opportunity presents itself, it will likely pass you by. Today is a good day to take the opportunity before you and put it into practice. Want a perfect photo? Go to a professional. But even a professional takes time to perfect your photo. It took Mom countless hours to create those extraordinary photos of my daughter. It didn't happen overnight, but when she completed the project set before her, she achieved perfection.

Many of us want results immediately, and when we don't get what we want in the allotted time we expect it, we give up trying. Why is that? If our car is in the shop, and it's not ready when they said it would be, there is nothing we can do about it. Many of us would like to sit down and throw a temper tantrum like a two-year-old, but even that is not going to change the facts. The only one who can change your situation is you, and you need to do so immediately—like right now. Do you even realize how much happiness you have forfeited because you have allowed some past experience to steal your present joy? The question is how much longer are you going to allow your past to reside over your future?

Do something positive for yourself. Take the time right now. Grab your favorite photo album, look through it, and take as much time as you want pondering over the memories of a lifetime. Now do yourself a favor: let the past be just that. Smile, laugh, and cry at yesterday and all those things you couldn't change. When you're done, close the album and live life in the here and now. The photographs of yesterday explain your history, those photos reflecting all the areas in your life you couldn't change, but you can live life better today because of the knowledge you gained from them. If you think this is impossible, there is someone who would love nothing more then to help you overcome your past. All you have to do is be willing and ask. Don't waste another day dwelling on what could have been; instead face tomorrow certain that present circumstances are subject to change. Someone who loves you above all things wants to do the impossible with your life. Why don't you allow Him to, and let Him start right now? ("And looking upon them Jesus said to them, 'With men this is impossible but with God all things are possible.'" (Matt. 19:26 New American Standard)

Scarred Tissue

Let's face the facts; no one actually wants to undergo a surgical procedure. Unfortunately though there are those times when there is no other option, and surgery becomes a necessity. Doctors often times try to rectify certain medical conditions by prescribing medication in an attempt to do everything humanly possible to keep the individual from facing the alternative. Several years ago, I found myself in this predicament. The doctor prescribed medicine to try to alleviate a persistent problem, but was unable to solve it. I reached the point where medicine no longer worked, and surgery was no longer an option but a requirement. The doctor went into great detail explaining what I was about to undergo and assured me he would do everything possible to minimize scarring.

My oldest daughter is fascinated with television shows that relate to crime scenes and how investigators reach their conclusions. She is especially interested in cases where the only things recovered are the unidentifiable remains of an individual. She watches closely as investigators try to frantically piece the life of the individual back together searching endlessly for anything that will give them a clue as to the identity of the remains that lie before them. Dental records are often a good indicator as to whom the individual might be, but in some cases a more extensive search is required. Studying the bones more closely, investigators may be able to detect what caused the person's death. Scarred bone tissue may tell investigators of a past injury or perhaps a history of abuse, leading investigators on an extensive search for a perpetrator in either case.

Now it's time for you to prepare yourself because I am about to dig so deep into your imagination that you are going to think I know something that perhaps I shouldn't. I am about to uncover something you thought would remain hidden forever. If you are the type person who is scared to face reality, maybe its best if you skip to chapter five right now, without reading the rest of this chapter. If there is one thing I've learned about people, it's that we tend to avoid thinking about the things that make us feel uncomfortable, make us lose control, or are currently controlling us. We believe that all will be well if we leave well enough alone. I write this as someone who doesn't know you but still cares deeply for your soul. Our past experiences can cause uncertainty to us as individuals. In order to comprehend this uncertainty, we must first understand where it originated.

Let's talk about those scars that can't be seen on the skins outer surface. Scars imbedded so deep within you that not even America's finest investigators can detect them. Scars that perhaps happened decades ago, yet still remain evident—only not to the naked eye. They're deep within your soul. What about those invisible scars that remain as though they where committed with a piercing instrument at the hands of a skilled professional? Scars no one—not even your husband, wife, or your closest family and friends—can detect because you've safely kept them hidden. Maybe until today even you had no idea they existed.

Maybe you're a mother who raised your children, never grasping why your own mother walked out on you, secretly hating her for her absence in your life. A husband who sacrificed all he was for the family he always wanted, only to lose them in a vehicle accident, despising the whole world because of your loss. Maybe today you're the grown woman who constantly hid from her abusive parents as a child and now wants nothing more then to watch them suffer endlessly in their old age. Perhaps you're just an ordinary girl, raped on that unsuspecting day, now walking in fear daily and wishing you were never born. Could you be the wife whose husband promised her forever but eventually broke that promise, hating him and categorizing all men because of his actions? Are you the mother and father sitting by as your little princess destroys herself with drugs and justify her actions by pointing fingers at the dealer instead of the doer?

I have not even begun to scratch the surface of those things that cause us to feel the depths of pain. We live in a world that was created wonderfully yet has no desire other than to self-destruct. Those things that we should be allowed to hold sacred are constantly being manipulated by a society out to destroy the human soul. Not one of the above incidents carries more weight than another or is of less importance because it was not mentioned. What we must realize is the uncertainty that we face today can stem from a wound that happened long before we had any control over those things that structured our lives. We have allowed the outer appearance of our being to cover up the scars that have so deeply hurt us. In doing so, we manipulate the world into believing all is well with us, when in fact a part of us may have died years before it was meant to.

Contemplate for a moment, those things that have happened in your life that may have left scars embedded in the inner depths of your soul. Maybe until today you didn't recognize them, and now they've been brought to light. Examine those things that have inflicted pain in you're life carefully and agree that some would have been much less painful if someone had literally taken a knife and cut us open without anesthesia. Sounds a bit gruesome, I know. But the fact remains, some of life's pain would have been much more tolerable had it of been inflicted that way. More importantly, you have been hurt—by whom or what remains buried deep within you. Perhaps you've shared your turmoil with someone you trusted or maybe you carry it alone, keeping it buried so you don't ever have to relive the agony again.

I am a firm believer that no one human being can comprehend the pain of another, we can relate to it; to say I share your pain is less than truthful. We each react to pain differently. I am physically tough; I can withstand physical pain that most humans would cringe at the thought of bearing. On the other hand, I suffer a great weakness in the emotional department: things that other people can withstand send me into an emotional frenzy. I cannot understand the extent of your bereavement any better than you can understand mine. I remember the death of my grandmother very vividly. I recall my parents telling us about her death and the days and weeks that followed. I remember crying a great deal and not being able to grasp that she was gone. On the other hand, my other siblings had already dealt with their grief. I am sharing this with you to let you know each of us handles situations differently, in our own way, and in our own time.

My intentions are not to reopen old wounds or cause you any amount of pain. Unfortunately, however, sometimes the only way to stop the effects of scarring is to expand the wound until its wide open and clean away any fragments that could hinder the healing process. Any situation that wounded you must be dealt with or healing will never occur. Hiding from your hurt, holding onto your pain, and wanting nothing more then revenge is hindering you from a lifetime full of promise. It is in our human nature to want to watch those who have done us harm suffer, believing that if I was hurt they should hurt also. Unfortunately it is not for you or me to decide the punishment of those who may have offended us. "Vengeance is mine and retribution. In due time their foot will slip; for the day of their calamity is near. And the impending things are hastening upon them." (Deut. 32:35 New American Standard)

Jesus also suffered severe scarring at the hands of others. As the Bible says, "For dogs have surrounded me. A band of evildoers has encompassed me. They pierced my hands and my feet." (Ps. 22:16 New American Standard). Understand that the scars that Jesus endured where on behalf of all those who have ever hurt you or you have ever hurt. None of us are above reproach. "I have not come to call the righteous, but sinners to repentance." (Luke 5:32 NIV) He allowed the infliction of great physical pain upon His body for the great inflictions you were going to have to bear or those burdens you may have inflicted on others. "For all have sinned and fall short of the glory of God." (Rom. 3:23 New American Standard)

It would be a great misconception to lead you to believe that Jesus didn't come for all those who have ever caused you pain. Are these words supposed to bring comfort to your soul? Probably not! But the truth remains, Jesus went to the cross for all of us: not just you or me but you, me, and everyone who ever meant us harm. Right now my intention is not to lead you to believe that your scars are not important, or that Jesus doesn't care that you've been hurt or carry a burden. I think it's only fair that you understand, He recognizes your pain, but He also came for the inflictor in the same manner He came for you.

With that said, I want you to understand that the injustice that was done to you may have caused you a great deal of pain, causing you to fight a battle that's not yours to fight. You have an advocate who sits at the right hand of the Father who is living proof that battles can be overcome, even if it looks as though the odds are stacked against you. An advocate is an intercessor, helper, or comforter. Jesus Christ is your advocate, and He wants to help you with your battle. Imagine, if you will, playing tug-of-war. Only two people are playing the game, one on either side of the rope. Eventually one overpowers the other, determining the winner. Now contemplate with me, if there are four players: two on either side of the rope. That's twice the strength, twice the power, and twice the opportunity of overcoming the odds. Think about your own personal struggle, the battle you've been fighting all alone. I am going to take a giant step and speak out in boldness. Your hurt, you've been hurt, and you're mad at everything and everyone who has ever had anything to do with your secret battle or who may have caused those hidden scars you carry. The tissue is so damaged that at times you have to shake yourself to alleviate the pain. At times the anger is so intense that you don't even recognize the individual looking back at you in the mirror. I could go on, but there's no need. You understand what it is that I am saying.

I have heard on several occasions that two is better then one. It seems like there are occasions when you are standing alone in battle, but keep in mind looks can be deceiving. There many stories of battles in the Bible where one man stands alone against what looks like unreasonable odds. David and Goliath is a story that comes to mind. David, a mere shepherd boy, confronts a giant named Goliath. Appearing much larger than David, Goliath mocks David. However, at the battle's end, David stands victorious over the giant, Goliath. Why? Because David did not go into battle alone, he went into battle with his advocate, his intercessor, his helper, the Lord God Almighty. I must take this opportunity to ask you, who are you taking into battle with you? Are you attempting to win with only one player on your side, that player being you? Are you attempting to overcome your battle without the right weapons in your arsenal? All the weapons of heaven are at your disposal, why aren't you using them? If you're fighting and it's just you and you alone, your battle will never be won, and your scar will forever be evident. Maybe today's leading investigators won't discover it, but it will remain just the same. I want you to have a fair fight. Yes, you've been in battle, the scars seem to be the evidence of defeat, and everything seems to point to the fact that you've lost the war.

This is going to hurt but it's something that must be said. In order to get over those things that caused us the initial hurts and pains, we must let them go. We have to stop dwelling on them. Easier said then done, I know. We cannot overcome anything or get past the pain of our hurt as long as we allow the pain to constantly overshadow everything that happens in our lives. If a dark cloud remains over the sun, everything in the vicinity of the cloud remains dark. But once the cloud passes, the sun shines brightly. As long as you allow the wound to remain open, it never has a chance to get well. Once you let it all go, only then can Jesus apply the salve to help you heal.

Stop right now, go in your room, shut the door, and look in the mirror. Really take a good hard look at yourself. I want you to concentrate on who you are and what you really want out of life. Cry if you must, laugh if you want. Stand there for as long as you need to. What I am about to say is extremely important, so listen carefully! The reflection staring back at you in the mirror is created in the image of God; your battle scars are as evident as Jesus Christ's were on Calvary. Your tears are being bottled up in heaven, and this very day the Lord God Almighty beckons you to let go. For once, don't hold anything back. Your advocate wants you to know that you don't have to fight this battle alone. He's been beside you every step of the way. When you could no longer walk, it was your comforter, your helper; it was He that carried you. You're His David, your problem His giant, and He is your Lord God Almighty. Do what He asks of you this day and give it to Him. Let it go. Then and only then will those scars become just a reflection of a battle won. David was not the only giant slayer in Gods arsenal; you can be too!

On The Flip Side

I am not, nor have I ever been, an avid football watcher. However, I seem to have surrounded myself with children who are enthused by a bunch of men chasing after a pigskin. I ask questions, trying to comprehend and expand my knowledge of the game and keep abreast of what has just occurred or what may possibly occur under the circumstances. Recently, we watched the game of all games: the Super Bowl. Totally engrossed in all the festivities leading up to the big game, I found myself waiting with anticipation as the day's events unfolded. Finally, the time had arrived for the big game. I attentively watched as several players from two of the best teams in the National Football League headed toward the center of the football field. I learned that the purpose of this meeting was to decide who would receive the ball and who would kick the ball off. That decision would be decided by the flipping of a coin. Sitting on the edge of their seats, those with us that night believed the fate of the game resided with the winner of the coin toss.

Raising children comes with its fair share of learning experiences. For example my children have taught me that each has their own opinion, each has their own likes and dislikes, and each identifies differently to certain things. I love my children, truly I do. If you're a parent you will appreciate what I am about to say. If your children are anything like mine, they are never wrong! When my children brought home report cards that might not have met with my approval, it was without a doubt "the teachers fault." When my son can't find his clothes, it's his sisters' fault or mine. My daughter is well-known for opening the refrigerator, looking inside, turning to me and saying, "Mom there's nothing in here to eat!" even when it's full of food. By no means am I condemning my children. They're my entire life, after God. I want you to understand the reality: things are not always as they seem, and like the coin tossed in air and its impact on the finale of the game, how each of us perceives our past or present circumstances could play a significant role in the outcome of our destiny on this walk called life!

Right now, I want to talk to all those who have ever had a hard time facing themselves in the mirror. I want to talk to all those who feel as though this book or any book like it was written for everyone else but them. I've written about overcoming obstacles, now I want to talk to all those who believe they stand on the outside looking in but never making an entry. Maybe you're not the one on the receiving end of a bad situation, but the individual who initiated the situation. Maybe you're not the abused, but the abuser. You might be the mother who walked out; the drunk driver who stole the family, destroying the dreams of a man; the reason a family separated or a child cries. Sometimes the hardest things in life to face are those things that cause us to cringe inwardly at the very thought of them.

I am by no means here to condone what you have done, nor am I here to condemn you. In most cases you have probably already condemned yourself enough for all of us. I can assure you it is not my place or anyone else's place to pass judgment upon you. Unfortunate for most, we live in a society that is not as forgiving as we would like them to be. We live in a society blessed with a free will, passing judgment and choosing whom to forgive has become a justifiable option rather than an exception as it is in the bible. Society braces itself against the accused in most all situations leaving absolutely no room for forgiveness. With a society set against you the accused, why should you believe that there is someone who loves you so much He sent His Son to die for you?

When Peter asked Jesus in Matthew 18:21, "Lord how many times shall I forgive my brother when he sins against me? Up to seven times?" Jesus replied, "I tell you not seven times but seventy-seven times." Wouldn't this scripture be wonderful if every one who ever read it took it to heart and put it into action? This may be a rule with which to live by, but many of us choose whom this rule should apply to. The concept of forgiveness is one of the greatest acts of humility and the hardest for most individuals to comprehend the importance of.

I could write this and lead you to believe that I have never offended anyone or been the accused, but then I would be misleading you. At this present time, I am forty-five, the mother of three children, and far from perfect. There were those times in my life when I did not care if there was a God, what He thought, or if He even existed. With the three characteristics listed above, I could hardly be perfect. In all honesty, He was of no concern to me. Living my life meant more to me then anything else. What am I trying to tell you? I write this as someone who was raised in the way she should go. Upon reaching adulthood, I wanted nothing more than to discover all that life had to offer. I didn't have a care in the world or who got hurt by my discovery process. In fact my life left a lot to be desired.

Can I relate to those who in one way or another think they are among the so-called unforgivable ones? Yes I can. Have I committed heinous crimes or done the unthinkable? No. But a sinner I am, saved by grace and grace alone. Even though I knew how much I needed God, I remained rebellious, not budging an inch even in my most desperate hours. I remember waiting on the results of a medical test. When the results came in they showed signs of abnormalities. After taking a high dose of medication, I had to be retested. In between that time, I called my mother and told her about the results of the first test. Being a firm believer in God, my mother advised me to ask God for help. I simply replied, "It makes me sick when people don't serve God yet call upon Him when they need Him." My mother ended the conversation with me by saying, "He would love to hear from you!"

Sinner—judged and condemned by a free-willed society—He would love to hear from you! It's hard to fathom: a God who met perfection in His Son Jesus Christ sending Him to die for the likes of you and me, but He did. I don't know what you've done or where you've been. Possibly you're sitting in a cell, paying the penalty for a crime committed or perhaps your being held captive in your very own private cell while living freely in society, haunted by a past full of regrets. It's safe to assume that wherever you stand in the present, those regrets of yesterday find a way of hindering your thoughts of the future. This is not written to be a constant reminder of what used to be but for you to seek solace in the hope that not all things are as they seem.

Consider this moment in time if you will: three crosses, two robbers—one on His right side, the other on His left side—and our Savior Jesus Christ in the center. One of the robbers hurtles insults at Jesus, the other robber asks Him to remember him when He gets to paradise. Both robbers committed crimes worthy of certain death yet hanging between them is the man without blemish sent to die on their behalf. Without a moment's hesitation, upon his asking, Jesus grants the man found guilty of committing a crime a pardon of sorts. He does not pass judgment, instead granting him the forgiveness he so desperately seeks, and a place in paradise. As the bible says:

> But the other answered and rebuking him said,
> "Do you not even fear God, since you are under
> the same sentence of condemnation?"

"And we are punished justly, for we are receiving what we deserve for our deeds, but this man has done nothing wrong."

And he was saying, "Jesus, remember me when You come in your kingdom!"

And He said to him, "Truly I say to you, today you shall be with Me in Paradise." (Luke 23:40–43 New American Standard)

In the eyes of God the Father, forgiveness is given to those who seek it with a sincere heart. Forgiveness is not only for a select few or for those who choose to serve Christ. I can only write based on what I have experienced. Anything else is merely fictional. God took me a sinner, granted me a pardon, and gave me a second chance to see all that life has to offer with a different perspective. How the free world passes judgment and analyzes forgiveness is no reflection as to the way that God the Father perceives it. Society busies itself with picking specs from the eyes of others. God busies Himself by looking for those who earnestly seek Him in faith. "And without faith, it is impossible to please Him for He who comes to God must believe that He is, and that He is a rewarder of those who seek Him." (Heb. 11:6 New American Standard)

Many believe that God would rather hear from those who have never done anything wrong and that God has no use for the individual linked to corruptible behavior. I take this opportunity to once again tell you that all have sinned and fall short of the glory of God. To say you are part of a select few is itself a lie of great magnitude. No matter how righteous one believes he or she is, before God the Father all appear as filthy rags. Are you so bad that God will not grant you the pardon you are so desperately in need of? Do you fear seeking Him, afraid that He to will shun you as the world has? My friend, I cannot be more honest with you then at this very moment, you cannot afford to wait and see if God looks at you as the world does. God does not act in accordance with what the world wishes. If you're waiting on the world to grant you your pardon, you will always be just that … waiting! Was it not the world that put our Lord and Savior Jesus Christ on the cross? Do you really think the world will pardon you?

There will always be those who will take their past regrets to the grave with them. Today however you have a choice; you may be behind bars in the tightest security prison in the world. Those bars may have you restrained, but don't allow them to hold you captive from the grace that is granted to each of us by our Heavenly Father. Perhaps you have your freedom, walking to and fro as you please, but inside you feel as though you're confined and freedom from your guilt is out of your reach. Perhaps you're feeling as though there's no hope because the world has set itself against you. May I take this opportunity to pass the words of my mother on to you, "He would love to hear from you!"

In the midst of despair, even the guilty robber knew that in his most desperate hour he needed something or someone.

Maybe you're hardcore, the tough type like the other robber who believed until the very end that you don't need anything or anybody. I'd like to take this opportunity to let you know that during that thieves most desperate hour his eyes were gouged out by a crow, this to his dreadful misfortune. For those of you who know you need something more then that which society grants, God the Father waits desperately to hear from you. The world may have picked up God's gavel and passed its sentence, judging you guilty, but in the end it's God who either grants the pardon or pronounces the sentence.

Right now you may be standing outside, have your hand on the door, contemplating turning the handle. Don't despair, for the God of mercy stands behind the most important door you will ever walk through. Grace is granted by God, not by a free-willed society. Friend, things are not always as they seem. The world may never forgive or forget, but God will. An opportunity of a lifetime has just presented itself to you. Will you forever stand outside looking in or will you enter as the robber did with a last minute decision made in a most desperate hour? Time is of the essence; your appeal has just been granted. My friend what you choose to do right now may forever play a determining factor in your eternal destination. The coin has landed, the decision made. Today you will receive the ball, what you do with it may forever decide your fate.

Possible Side Effects

Everything we buy today seems to come with some sort of warning label. Labels on products distribute information to keep the consumer from misusing a product. A warning label placed on certain products is used as a precautionary measure to help you avoid a hazard that may otherwise cause harm to you or your family. There are those labels that cause us to chuckle, and there are those that cause us to worry about the product we are about to consume or use. It seems at times that the potential side effects from the use of a particular product are far worse then the purpose for which the product was initially intended. In any case, labels are placed on products to protect the buying public from the dangers that surround the item purchased. Wouldn't life be great if it came with a set of warning labels that warned us of the potential dangers that lie ahead, in the wake of our decisions?

There is nothing I like more then my children coming home from school and telling me they have a school project to complete and that the deadline for completion is quickly approaching. Their school projects usually require my assistance or in most cases require me to attempt them solo. Recently, I had the pleasure of making a catapult, which is one of a number of mechanical devices used to throw a projectile (golf ball, marble, tennis ball etc.) a great distance. Careful to follow the verbal instructions given, I began to construct the catapult accordingly. Spending almost an entire day building and rebuilding this catapult, I was finally content with the results of the completed project before me. Smiling with delight, I was ready to test my project. My verbal instructions were brief regarding the construction of the catapult, and I was unaware of some very important facts concerning this project. This catapult was without a doubt in need of some hazard warnings. Unaware of these warnings, I prepared for a test run, using a golf ball as my projectile. I pulled back on the catapult's arm and released my grip. I will tell you that the golf ball went the distance required and beyond, but I will keep to myself what the golf ball destroyed before it reached its final destination. I assume, had I read the directions rather than taking them verbally, I would have saved myself the purchase of a piece of glass, the countless hours of building and rebuilding, and the embarrassment of telling my children that their project was completed but that completed project came at the expense of a valuable lesson. Reading and following the directions can save you from the possibility of suffering potentially dangerous side effects.

How enchanted would our lives be without side effects of any kind? What if, for example, marriage came with a certificate of authenticity and was unbreakable under any circumstances? Wouldn't it be great if our children were born with a satisfaction guarantee—healthy, happy, and never causing us a moment's grief—or we could return them until satisfaction is met? What if our finances came with an unlimited amount of resources at our fingertips any hour of the day or night? Or if old age would set in with grace, no aches or pains, and knowledge stored in a never-forget memory bank? Or how about if death came with immediate occupancy, no suffering, no prolonged illness, and all life's trials forever forgotten as we slip off to sleep and into eternity? One could not ask for much more then that: a happy marriage, perfect children, unlimited financial resources, old age setting in without complications, and eventually a peaceful death.

I don't have to tell you life is not that simple; there are plenty of side effects that interfere with our day-to-day living. Life is full of experiences: some we wish we could have avoided others we would not have missed for the world, and those we haven't even begun to experience. Each experience has or will affect our lives in one way or another! Where would we be had such occurrences not transpired in our lives? It has taken me some time to realize, but I know I have become the person I am because of the side effects I've lived through. God initially molded us in our mother's wombs, but it's those experiences that God has allowed us to pass through or those we brought upon ourselves that builds character and defines who we are. "For you created my inmost being; you knit me together in my mother's womb." (Ps. 139:13 NIV)

Occurrences transpiring in our lives brought on by reckless decision making have the power to hamper our resolve and channel our efforts toward a thoughtless act of indulgence without contemplating the consequences of our actions. A hindrance in the life of an individual interrupts the function of our ability to perform to the best of our potential. An impediment of any great magnitude can cause the life of the individual to spiral downward affecting not only themselves but all those around them. Possible side effects caused from an obstruction can destroy not only the individual's life but his or her family as well. Take a moment right now and think of a time when you made a major decision concerning yourself or your family. Did you analyze the situation from all angles? Or did you do what was best for you? If you chose the latter, what side effects did you or your loved ones suffer? I make the major decisions in my household; there have been those times when my vote was the only one that mattered, and many times my decisions caused serious repercussions for my family and friends.

Maybe you're in the middle of making a decision and don't think that anyone will be effected by your choice. I am not referring just to the financial decisions in your life, although they are extremely important. I am talking about those life-changing decisions: The marriage that's in trouble and the temptation of the pretty secretary at the office or the handsome new boss who started last week. The decision to play the lottery rather then paying the past-due mortgage. The decision to send the child support check or spend the money cultivating a new relationship. Perhaps it's easier for you to turn a blind eye rather then acknowledging the fact that your child has a behavior problem. Whether you choose to address a situation by either acting upon it or ignoring its existence, there is an extremely good chance that someone will be affected by your actions or the lack there of. Could it be that you never anticipated the consequences for the actions that you have already taken or those you are currently contemplating? Today is a very good day for you to take into consideration the possibility of a warning label being placed on those things you decide to do. It is imperative that you reflect upon the possible side effects that your decisions may cause to those with whom you say I love you to at days end.

God anointed David king at a very young age. When the time came for David to become king, he had it all: money, power, popularity, good looks, but even all that was not enough to keep him content. He wanted the wife (Bathsheba) of another (Uriah). David sent for Bathsheba and took what did not belong to him. The consequence or side effect of King David's careless act of self-gratification cost his family dearly, so much so that David's house would never again be the same. (2 Sam. 12:1–15 NIV) I suggest you take a few minutes to consider reading that which God poured upon the household of David for his actions paying strict attention to verses 10–12. Perhaps your decision may not be that of David's but those concerning improper business ethics or compromising your moral beliefs. Is the compromise you make today worth the consequence you or your family may have to endure tomorrow?

Before you make a compromising decision that may change your household, try this first. Take out a sheet of paper. Fold it in half the long way and on one side, write positive side effects and on the other side, write negative side effects. Do not overlook the negative side effects to gratify yourself; this is your family after all! Write everything that comes to mind. Don't erase any answers, after all you wrote them for a reason. Don't just sit there and write for a few minutes and then say, "I'm done." Do this over a long period, allowing time to bring to mind all plausible effects either good or bad. Pray about the decision and ask God to bring to mind both the positives and the negatives of the decision that you must make. After allowing a period of time to pass, compare the negatives to the positives. If you have honestly written all of both categories down, consider this: is the compromise worth it? Is the decision in the best interest of all those who will be affected by your choice? I hope so!

Regardless of the actions David—the apple of Gods eye—chose, God still loved him unconditionally. God is not a God who won't forgive; He will. But He is also the God of judgment, the God of wrath, and the God of vengeance. Forgiveness does not exempt us from suffering the consequences of our actions. Our flesh will tempt us with menial desires. There are those of us who feel we cannot resist. After all, David couldn't, and he was appointed by God Himself. So why should we? God gave us David as an example. He rose to be a great man that fell into temptation. David saw the wrong of his ways, and he was forgiven. What David didn't do was take into consideration the consequences brought on by his wishes to self-gratify. His decision to satisfy his desire caused his family to endure side effects they may have never had to. Being king did not exempt David or his family from suffering the wrath of God. All because as head of his household, David made a choice, and he could do nothing about his decision once he had acted upon it. In the end, all David could do was look onward, realizing the true cost of his actions, and the affect it had on those who he loved.

I write this as someone who made decisions that caused serious side effects to those around me. Egotistical acts of self-indulgence are costly. If I could have looked through an hourglass and been able to see the outcome of my decisions, I am sure I would have acted differently! How about you? The ability to change those things of yesterday is not ours, but the choice to change tomorrow is. Consider carefully all the options before compromising all those who will endure the potentially dangerous side effects from self-centered decision making.

"Pictures are worth a thousand words," what do you see when looking at yours? Looking into a puddle that has accumulated after a rain, who do see looking back at you? Perhaps you're ashamed to look at yourself because of what you've become in light of decisions made. You're not the only one who's ever made a careless decision but what you must realize now is that others may be suffering because of your actions. Redeem yourself like David did. Think, "I've made a mistake, Lord. I know you love me unconditionally, please forgive me." Don't wait; don't put if off. Don't self indulge another day, for the pleasures you enjoy today may be coming with a price tag you can't afford later! "For those whom the Lord loves He disciplines, and He scourges every son whom He receives. It is for discipline that you endure. God deals with you as with sons, for what son is there whom his father does not discipline?" (Heb. 12:6–7 New American Standard)

From The Pew

This is where the book takes an interesting turn. There are some extraordinary things that transpire during a Sunday morning church service. There are the usual things that happen from week to week, like Mrs. So and So coming into church and claiming her regular seat, Mr. What's His Name who seems to fall asleep like clockwork every Sunday, the lady who sits behind you who hits all the high notes off key, or the children who have to use the bathroom every couple of minutes during the hour-long service. If you've ever experienced a church service, you can relate to the above items. Every once in a while an extraordinary situation occurs, like when the preacher thinks he's delivering the message of a lifetime but can't understand why his congregation is sitting there with smug little smiles covering their faces. It is not until after the service has ended that he realizes his pants were unzipped the whole time he was preaching. By no means am I downplaying the importance of a church service; I'm just assessing those things that can be seen from the pew!

You may find that as you continue to read this book, you asking yourself, "Is she by chance referring to me?" Understand that I do not mean to criticize you or your core beliefs but to cause you to examine the importance of how you appear in the eyes of others. I have heard it said on many occasions that the worst people to serve in restaurants on any given Sunday is the church crowd. You may find it hard to believe that—right after coming from the pew—one would act obnoxious, but believe it or not it happens. I am a firm believer that people who are known churchgoers face harsher criticisms then those who don't attend church at all.

What happens when you get up from the pew and walk away from a church service into the hours or days ahead? If people were to examine your daily walk, would they be able to tell you even sat in a pew at all? A high school teacher once told me that if I was ever going to succeed in life, I must be able to take criticism. Constructive criticism opens the eyes of an individual or closes them completely. Criticism is an adjustment in our lives that we would much rather live without. After all, we have to accept criticism at work and at home, but do we have to accept criticism in our spiritual walk as well? Look at it this way, this may or may not pertain to you. If it does, you may want to make a few adjustments. If it does not, stand tall and walk proudly; you're among a select few.

Over the past several years, I have had the pleasure of ministering to teens and young adults. Some would say I am half crazy. After all, teenagers think they have all the answers, they talk back, and they only need you when they want something. From the very beginning of my ministry, I laid down the ground rules: don't lie to me, if you need me for anything call me, and above all know that I don't play when I pray! Sounds simple enough and over time I have come to earn the respect and trust of these young people. So much so that I have attended court hearings on their behalf, spoken with probation officers, and taken kids to weekly court-appointed classes. By no means am I saying that all the kids with whom I have come in contact are in trouble, but some have found themselves involved in alternative extra-curricular activities that had some consequences. My desire was nothing more then to show these children the love of God at any cost. Several have come and gone from my life, but every now and again one of my teenagers' returns as a young adult to tell me his or her story. Below is one such story.

The name below is fictitious however the story is true. Ken was the kid next door, his family moved in, and he immediately became friends with my two girls. They went to school together, played together, and more often then not, he was a regular at the dinner table. Ken was eight when we first met. He was a chubby little fellow who was afraid of my youngest daughter, and she liked it that way. Several years later, Ken moved to a new home just down the street from ours. We saw less and less of him, eventually to the point of seeing him once a month. On one of these visits we found that Ken and his family were again moving, this time to a different city. "Keep in touch," we said as we watched Ken and his family move away once more. Time moved on, and like all things, so did we. Every now and then my family and I would reminisce about the old days and wonder what ever became of Ken.

Years passed, and I ran into Ken, no longer the kid of yesterday, but now a man. Visible to the naked eye were the changes Ken had made with his life; his heart was hidden behind a now hardened exterior. With the pleasantries behind us, the masquerade Ken hid behind started to diminish once I reminded him that this was me he was talking to and that no matter what, I loved him unconditionally. Ken joined us for dinner like old times and began to unfold the lost years of his life. As the tears welled up in his eyes and began to slide down his cheeks, Ken struggled to look at me, as he murmured through quivering lips "Mrs. B, I owe you everything!" Ken owed me nothing. But the sincerity in his words motivates me to continue on today.

"When I left you," he started, "I got involved in drugs, gangs, violence, and stuff I should not have been involved in. Mrs. B.," he said, "I saw stuff." By now the tears where running as though a faucet had been turned on. "I saw a girl almost beaten to death over a drug deal that had gone bad," we sat in silence as we waited for Ken to gain his composure, and then he continued.

He went on to tell us how he tried to get away from the trouble, to get away even to the point of camping out in the woods to hide. "They still found me," he said, "You see, Mrs. B., when you're involved like I was, you can't hide because trouble finds you." He went on to tell us that when he was hiding, he thought about the things I taught him, how God loves him no matter what, "Just like you do, Mrs. B" he said. (What Ken didn't realize is that God loves him much more then I do.) When Ken was alone, scared, and in hiding, he decided he needed to make a change in his life. He decided it was time to go back to the only place he felt safe, really safe. Ken made a decision to go to church. The following Sunday, he took a friend and together they entered a hospital of sorts for sick people: they went to church.

"Going in and finding a seat was easy. What was not easy were the stares, the nods of distaste, the mother who moved her child away from us as we sat down. Mrs. B., we really wanted to make a change in our life, we listened to the message, and at the end of the service when they had an alter call, both my friend and I went down. I can only speak for myself," Ken said. "I wanted to lay it all down before God, everything I had ever done; I wanted to surrender all of who I had become over to God. My friend," Ken continued "went into church with drugs and a gun in his pocket, truly feeling sorry for what he had done with his life. He reached inside his pocket and pulled out the gun and drugs and laid them on the altar. He fell on his knees and begged for God's forgiveness. As soon as my friend laid the gun and drugs down on the altar, the church pews emptied. People got up from their seats and left the building. When we got up and turned to leave, we did not need to be told we were not welcome back by those who remained inside the church. We could see it in the looks on their faces.

"Mrs. B., we never did go back, and I never will again." That was the last thing Ken said to me. Since our conversation that night, the little boy of yesterday is now a man paying for his choices. Ken found his way back into my life only long enough to share his story. He now sits in a maximum-security prison serving time for his decisions. When I saw the paper with his photo plastered on the front page, the article reading, "Florida's Most Wanted," I wondered if perhaps there were not other measures I could have taken to prevent such an outcome. Ken, if you ever read this book, my love for you has not changed. I am disappointed by your actions, but I love you today, more then yesterday but never as much as tomorrow. And Ken your Heavenly Father loves you so much more then me.

I am sure that some of you will agree with the actions that the above body of believers took. We live in a society that believes guns, drugs, and violence have no place in a church setting. In light of recent church shootings, it is highly understandable why people from the pew would react in such a way. On the other hand, preachers stand before congregations Sunday after Sunday, preaching messages of faith, hope, and love. In light of the continuous church messages about love and the numerous scripture references about God's unconditional love, how do the Kens of this world fit in to God's plan of forgiveness? Are we unwilling to share the grace and mercy granted to us by our Heavenly Father to them?

In your own personal walk have you ever imitated the actions of the above body of believers, moving away from a sinner who wants nothing more then the same forgiveness God granted to you? Ever give a look of distaste to people who don't look quite the way we expect them to? I personally have watched people get up and move from a pew because they had a problem with an individual who sat down next to them to worship the same God they did. Ladies and gentlemen, this is where the constructive criticism starts to hurt. If we as Christians initiate this sort of behavior from the pew, who then are we to complain when the church pews are empty on Sunday mornings? Why complain when family members analyze our life as a Christian and refuse to enter a church service because of it, or when a loved one passes, we assume their whereabouts, never contemplating that we may have played a role in their destiny?

God is not glorified by our attendance in church; it is what we do with the Kens of this world that brings glory to Him. Ken is just one story in a world of many, but his journey in particular causes me to reflect upon my own personal walk. One of the greatest commands Jesus left us with was to love—not love some, not love just a little, not love just a select few. He calls each of us to love unconditionally—just as He loves us— not just to love those we know or those with whom we meet regularly with on Sunday. "If you love those who love you, what reward will you get? Are not even the tax collectors doing that? And if you greet only your brothers, what are you doing more than others? Do not even pagans do that?" (Matt. 5:46–47 NIV)

Mine was not to justify Kens choices in life, the path he chose to walk down was surely his own doing. Mine is however to cause each of us to reflect upon our own personal walk, whether we're walking toward the Lord or causing someone to walk away from Him by our actions. Please understand I am not condemning those who walked away because of Ken's friends' choice to bring drugs or a gun to church. I am, however, putting forth the idea that each of us should examine ourselves the next time a stranger walks across our path or sits in our pew. Can someone tell you attended church on Sunday by watching your walk on Monday? Only you can answer that question!

Ken, if by chance you're reading this, I will again remind you that the God who formed you so long ago still holds you in the palm of His hand. You have the power to choose Him. God has the power to do all things, but he won't make you choose Him. That is a choice only you can make. Long before time began, God made a choice, creating you with a purpose in mind, and chose to love you unconditionally. Ken it may seem that God has moved so far away from you, but I must be honest with you, it is not He that's moved. He is in the same place you left Him, and He loves you and awaits your return. I promise! Please forgive me my dearest Ken, if in someway I have personally failed you. I love you dearly, and unconditionally, but God the Father loves you far more then I ever could or will. Seek solace in knowing that God will never look at you with our eye's but with His, and He will never love you according to our standards, but by the only standard He has ever professed and that is totally, without condition.

Obstacle Course

"Friday is field day and I am on the red team," my son yells as he comes running in the house after school. Excitement continues to build with each day that passes as Friday nears. I make it a habit of attending field day with my children; it's the only day I can make kids laugh at school without getting them in trouble. Field day is unlike any other day of the year. There are a multitude of games planned for all the kids to play, and of course a little competition between the red team and the blue team. The wet sponge relay, the tug of war, and the infamous obstacle course are among a few of the high-priority games for these young, competitive students. The obstacle course, as the most competitive event, is the center of everyone's attention on this particular Friday in spring. Hula-hooping; jumping up, over, and under a desk; skipping rope; running back; and tagging hands with the next competitor draws enthusiastic shouts of excitement from the children as they wait with anticipation to see whether the red or blue team will become victorious.

Obstacle courses are used in several different manners and for several different purposes. Military personnel, for example, familiarize new recruits with obstacle courses as a way of teaching them tactical movements for combat. Reality TV shows use obstacle courses to reveal the physical endurance of some of the world's finest athletes who compete for prizes, notoriety, and the ability to conquer feats unreachable by most. Family-orientated fun centers house obstacle courses as a way of allowing families the opportunity to work together as a team to defeat the obstacles placed before them, hindering them from completing the course. The sole purpose of an obstacle course is to cause the individual to use measures he or she may not use under ordinary circumstances with the determination to conquer the course. No greater achievement does one feel then the satisfaction one gets when reaching the finishing line after conquering a course riddled with obstacles.

Would it be safe to assume that this walk called life can be considered an obstacle course of sorts? Looking at life from infancy until one reaches adulthood, one can easily see that no two courses are charted the same. From infancy through childhood, we primarily depend on others. A child reaching his or her teenage years soon discovers that those things that were once handed to them must now be earned. A teenager reaching adolescence soon realizes his or her priorities must be put into perspective. The reality of dependency on others comes to a complete halt as the adolescent reaches adulthood. From the time one reaches the course of independence, many obstacles have been placed in the path of his or her life. Is it possible to conquer this course called life and still come out satisfied with oneself upon completing it?

Days, weeks, and years can pass untouched by life's events. However, without hesitation and at a moment's notice, an unexpected perplexity rears its head and challenges us to remain on course. Suddenly we find ourselves in the middle of this course called life with an obstacle placed directly in the center of our path, its main focus to undermine our success. Unexpected obstacles have a tendency to interfere with our ability to stay focused, prevent us from seeing past the obstacle, and hinder us from crossing the finish line. No amount of physical training can prepare us for these untimely incidents. Like athletes who pursue fitness, we to must prepare ourselves to defeat obstacles placed in our paths that keep us within inches of reaching the finish line.

Every athlete I have ever witnessed dresses appropriately for his or her sport. We are no different. What we wear into the arena may play an important role in helping us conquer the obstacles in our way. Our Heavenly Father loves us so much that He equipped each of us with a suit of armor that will help us defeat every obstacle placed in our path today, tomorrow, and forever. A gladiator cannot compete without physical endurance, our military cannot conquer without proper training, and you and I cannot undermine Satan's futile attempts at destruction if we are not prepared, well equipped, and dressed for battle.

Put on the full armor of God so that you can take your stand against the devil's schemes (Eph. 6:11 NIV). The obstacles that stand in between you and the finish line are devised by the one who would love nothing better then to watch you get off the course and give up, Satan. The struggle is not against flesh and blood, but against the ruler, against the authorities, against the powers of this dark world, and against the spiritual forces of evil in the heavenly realms. (Eph. 6:12 NIV) If you find yourself overwhelmed, feeling as though you're falling off course, and have no fight left in you, hold on because you have weapons at your disposal. In Ephesians 6:14–17 NIV, we are advised to put on the full armor of God, the belt of truth, the breastplate of righteousness, the gospel of peace, the shield of faith, the helmet of salvation, and the sword of the Spirit. Get back on course, my friend; God did not leave us defenseless. All the weapons of Heaven are at our disposal. All we have to do is use them.

I think it is important to note what a weapon is. A weapon is something to fight with; anything used or designed to be used, in destroying, defeating or injuring an enemy. God did not intend for us to travel down this course called life without any way of defeating obstacles or defending ourselves. A soldier going into battle without his or her weapon stands a very little chance of survival. How is it then that we feel we can stay on this course called life without arming ourselves with the proper equipment with which to complete it? Perhaps we take for granted with whom it is that we do battle or the need for weapons at all.

Let me introduce you to Lucifer, one of God's most trusted angels. Lucifer was a beautiful angel and a powerful one as well. He was so charming that he was able to persuade a third of the angels in heaven to rebel against God. See, Lucifer was not satisfied with his position in God's kingdom; he wanted more, much more. Lucifer wanted the kind of power that only God could posses. Lucifer wanted God's job and God's authority. But what Lucifer wanted most was to rule God's kingdom, which means Lucifer wanted sole control over our lives. God, The Father, wouldn't have it; He cast Lucifer and his angels out of heaven and into hell. Lucifer became known as Satan.

Satan has been throwing obstacles in the way of God's people ever since his abrupt departure from heaven. Satan wants nothing more then to lead us to believe that the obstacles he has placed in our path cannot be moved. I am here to tell you that Satan will continue to lead you and me off track and astray as long as we allow him to. The obstacle that is presently placed between you and the finish line was placed there by a fallen angel. Satan rebelled against God. Do you actually think he cares about you or your life? Do you think Satan cares whether you finish the course or not? Satan doesn't, but God does. It's time to tell Satan to get behind you. You have a course to finish, and you can do it, in Jesus's name.

Whatever course you find yourself walking down, God has prepared a weapon at your disposal and a course of action to follow. He will be with you every step of the way. It may seem at times as though God has left you alone to defeat the obstacles set before you or that he has deserted you for another. Take heart my friend. Be strong and courageous. Do not be afraid because the Lord your God goes with you; He will never leave you nor forsake you. (Deut. 31:6 NIV) Get up my friend, dust yourself off, put on your armor, and know this day that the Lord your God goes with you!

Looking across the obstacle course planned for my eight-year-old son, I see that his only concern is the complexity of the course set before him. His primary focus is completing the course and coming out victorious at day's end. As a parent, I desperately try to comfort my son by reassuring him that the course looks harder then it actually is. I look at him with affirmation when he looks back at me, assuring him that he can complete the course before him despite the obstacles in his way. Standing on the sideline, unable to help him complete the task at hand, I cheer him on believing that he will conquer the course regardless of what obstacle stands before him and the finish line.

Peering over the course of life before you now, does the course look a bit overwhelming? Perhaps it would be easier for you to step off the course or maybe if you could just turn around and go back. Maybe you believe anything would be easier than having to face the obstacles placed before you. From one friend to another, if you turn around now, you will turn around the rest of your life. I know turning around looks easier and probably hurts a lot less, but friend, turning and walking in the opposite direction doesn't move the obstacle, it moves you further away from reaching a goal. Like my son, I cannot help you finish the obstacle course before you. I can tell you though those obstacles placed in your path were put there by a fallen angel in an attempt to deceive you into thinking that you've gone as far as you're going to go on this course. It's up to you to prove him wrong.

God gave us a suit of armor to wear in preparation for this obstacle course called life. We should dress ourselves accordingly, not only applying those things that enhance our beauty. We should also apply daily those things that will ensure our safety against the enemy's attempts of disrupting our lives or keeping us from conquering a course. Something you should note perhaps write down and commit to memory. Every weapon God equipped us with—the breastplate of righteousness, the belt of truth, the gospel of peace, the shield of faith, the helmet of salvation, and the sword of the spirit—is ours to use as a defense against the obstacles that find themselves placed in life's pathway.

No matter what path you find yourself currently walking down, God did not intend for you to walk it without armor, without a course of action, or without Him. God has not left you, nor has He forsaken you. Face this obstacle course called life with the assurance that God is in control. God gave you the weapon with which to conquer the course. Even if it looks like the course is overwhelming, hold on! The greatest assurance that each of us has is to know that there is no greater weapon to guard our backsides from our enemies' attempts to throw us off course than God Himself. God did not design a weapon for our back, my friend, because He wanted that job solely for Himself.

The course called life is laid out before you, but your estimated time of arrival is up to you. I would be lying to say that

Satan will not lay obstacles in your path to keep you from reaching your destination. Can one complete this course called life successfully? By all means! Dress yourself accordingly and stay on course despite all obstacles. You can do it! Rest assured knowing that you have the greatest conqueror of all times watching your back, God the Father.

Negative vs. Positive

"You're a loser! You're no good at anything! You're not worth the air you breathe! You're an idiot! You will never amount to anything! Sometimes I wish you were never born!" Negativity spoken over time never stops affecting the heart and begins to consume the mind until one day it changes an individual's life forever. At some point the individual stops hearing the negativity and starts believing it. As ironic as it might sound, eventually the individual whose mind has been consumed with negative thoughts begins to live life as though no truer words have ever been spoken.

I must admit that I look at life through negative eyes. I meet life's situations with negativity before I ever see anything positive stemming from them. My first response in most situations is to think "never." I'll never meet these bills. I'll never finish this job. I'll never be thin. I'll never live happily ever after. Unfortunately, my list of negative responses is endless! I have come to realize that the more negative that I am, the more miserable I become. My negativity affects my attitude. It also affects how I react in situations, and I am a firm believer that my negativity affects the outcome of the circumstance. From experience, I can tell you negative thoughts reek of negative results.

Our Heavenly Father does not use condescending words in a negative tone. He does not berate us, nor does He look at us or our situation with negativity, and quite frankly, neither should we. I believe that we insult God the Father when we look at life with negativity instead of meeting life's challenges with a positive attitude. I have come to realize that negative situations can become a positive challenge for each of us if we approach them as such. Can something positive come from something negative? Positively!

Starting her sophomore year in high school, my daughter filled her schedule with Advance Placement (AP) classes. Her goal was to excel in those classes in the hopes of reaching at least high honors when it came time to graduate. From the very beginning, she met challenges in her AP biology class. In fact, the challenges became so intense that as a concerned parent I felt the need to meet with the teacher to see if I could alleviate some of my daughter's concerns, her primary concern being the ability to keep her grade point average (GPA) up. I was skeptical before I ever entered the conference room and much to my dismay skepticism did not escape me following the meeting. The teacher illustrated the importance of the quantity of work she administered and the scale on which she intended to grade my daughter's work, and she did not hesitate when she said, "If your daughter cannot keep up, she can drop the class like so many have before her."

My daughter, who was also called into the meeting, heard everything the teacher had to say. She sat there coherent yet on the verge of tears. Being sure to make eye contact with the teacher, I informed her that my daughter was not a quitter. Although skeptical, I assured the teacher that no matter how tough she became, my daughter would meet the challenge and excel in spite of it. I knew that my daughter would never consider dropping the class even though I suggested it. From that day forward, my daughter poured her heart and soul into that class, determined to show the teacher she could and would excel in spite of her negative remarks.

During the rest of her tenure at that high school, my daughter selected the same teacher in the hopes of achieving and excelling in high school academics. My daughter graduated with a 4.4 GPA and was salutatorian of her class. Her AP Biology teacher, who was also my daughter's senior class sponsor, sat yards away with nothing but admiration for her as she delivered her graduating speech with the same determination she had when she sat in that negative meeting. Sitting there in the stands listening to my daughter, my heart filling with pride. I realized it's the attitude with which we choose to approach those adversities that come our way that allows us to overcome obstacles, excel, and surpass even our own expectations.

Why share that with you? Perhaps all your life, you have heard nothing but negative words spoken about you. Maybe at the mention of your name you, you withdraw believing that once again you've done something that meets with someone's disapproval. Are you the child desperately trying to win the approval of a parent but repeatedly meeting disapproving results? Have you felt the negativity so much that you've begun to train yourself to act according to it instead of acting in spite of it? Could it be that you share the same negative attitude that I have? Maybe so many things have transpired in your life that show signs of negativity that you believe you were created to let life fall by the wayside and your bound into accepting things as they are. Stop right *now*!

My mom and dad have been married for forty-six years as of this writing. Over that period of time, things have physically changed between the two of them. If you asked my father if he could change anything about mom right now what would it be? My father's response would be absolutely nothing. In spite of the years that have passed and the changes that have physically taken place, my dad views my mother as aged to perfection. Perhaps you're the son, the daughter, the wife, the mother, the husband, or the father whose life has been so filled with negativity that you feel as though your heart has been taken out, stepped on, and then placed back inside your chest.

Maybe no one has ever taken the time to tell you or looked at you like my dad looks down at my mom, but right now, my friend, your Heavenly Father is looking down at you. Regardless of what any body has ever told you or anyone has ever said about you, in the eyes of God's the Father, *perfection has been met*! The way my father looks at my mom and God looks at you is different from how my mom looks at herself. I believe if you asked my mother if there was anything she could change about herself, "what would it be" and "would you change it given the opportunity?" I believe her answer would be "yes". Why? Because who would not change something about him or herself given the opportunity? See, my friend, when my father's eyes meet with my mothers all he can see is perfection in spite of what she thinks of herself. When God the Father looks down from heaven at what He has created, all He can see far surpasses perfection, despite what you've ever been told or what you have ever thought about yourself. Your God loves you like no other. You were His creation. He took His time and created you in His image, and nothing about you met with His disapproval. You are absolutely His best creation—of that I am positive!

"If what you're saying is true, why then did I have to suffer at the hands of others? If I am perfect as you say in God's eyes, why does He allow those things to come into my life that cause so much pain, that show signs of negativity? If God is *Soul'D Out* in love with me as you say, where is He when I need Him most?" Oh, my friend, you are not asking questions I have not asked myself time and again. I am merely a writer not the mind of God, but I want to give you something to hope for, a goal to reach for, like my daughter who prevailed when the odds were overwhelming against her. Perhaps you and I too can exceed even our own expectations while reaching for our ultimate destiny.

Ponder over these thoughts with me. Could it be that without negativity in our lives we would cease having a need for God? If our lives were absolutely perfect—happy home, good kids, healthy families, good jobs, and a perfect marriage—what plausible reason would we need God for? See, I believe that God allows some of those negative things to transpire in our life to keep us in touch with Him. If we were to be truly honest with ourselves, if everything that transpired in our life never met with a negative result would we even mention the name, give credit to, or call upon the God who created us? In all honesty, I don't believe we would! We would soon attribute our achievements to self-preservation, never identifying with the fact that it was a higher being that was behind our success.

God in all His infinite wisdom will never allow us to be self-made men and women. Allowing the negatives into our lives is God's way of letting you know He is still there, ready, willing, and able to help you overcome those adversities that have held you bound far longer then they should have. I don't know how you grew up or what your home life is like, maybe from the very beginning of time your life was surrounded by negativity. Perhaps as a child you heard it so much you accepted it and carried it along with you into adulthood. I am here to tell you, you've carried it long enough. Maybe so much negativity has transpired in your life that you've grown to accept it. My friend, we've accepted more then we needed to, and now it's time to give it to the One whose shoulders were made to carry a burden not fit for ours but for His and His alone.

Won't you give it to Him today? As I sit here and write this to you, I find it ministering to me. You see, I too have been held

Things To Do Today

WHEN GOD CLOSES

A DOOR AND OPENS

A WINDOW WELL

SOMETIMES OUT OF

NOWHERE HE'll DO

YOU ONE BETTER

HE'll KICK A

WHOLE WALL
DOWN

ound a way into my
ether. We can sit here
s, or we can free our-
tives into something
minds those thoughts
into the heavens and
at His creation. Let's
ant for us to carry yet

ed negativity into my
and keep me bound.
ore. My shoulders are
longer then I should
n you created me, all
hat it is that you see
re will be times when
learn what you want
help me to meet them
or loving me enough
m, oh Lord, take this
.

The Debt

I am a firm believer that the older individuals are, the wiser they are. I love to listen to my father when he tells stories of days gone by or stresses the importance of wisdom gained from years of experience. When a topic of conversation centers on something he is familiar with, he usually begins by saying, "Listen to me." The national debt is one such topic! "My children, your children, and your grandchildren will never be able to pay off the national debt!" My father says this with so much enthusiasm in his voice that it's hard to dispel what he is saying as anything less then truth. "How can you keep robbing Peter to pay Paul and expect to ever lower the national debt?" I listen attentively to what he has to say and contemplate how this will one day affect the future of my children and my grandchildren. According to AskQuestion. org, "As of June 26, 2008, the national debt is 9.4 trillion dollars." Is it even a possibility that this debt will ever be paid in my lifetime or the lifetimes of my children or my grandchildren?

I am only speaking for myself, but I am sure many can relate when I say, "I'm in debt!" I love to have things that are nice, but like most I realize nice things come with a price tag that surpasses my weekly income yet fit into my monthly budget. I am sure I am not alone. After all, people around the world seek comfort in acquiring those things that make them feel better and look better. Is there anything wrong with that? Not at all! Many have said, "I feel as though I've just signed my life away," after signing papers for their latest purchases. Plastic has become a lifestyle for many of us who desire to acquire. However, when we decide to purchase those things that make us happy, we are in debt and expected to pay until the debt is paid in full and satisfaction met. Unfortunately for most, myself included, the desire to acquire has left us in debt for years to come.

Have you ever co-signed a loan for someone? Perhaps you were trying to help them get their first start in life, or maybe someone was down on their luck and you wanted to help them. As a co-signer, you agreed to be the person responsible to finish paying the debt in the event the individual reneged on his or her obligation. Ever find yourself in this situation and get stuck paying for something you really didn't want? Did you feel angry, hurt, or regretful?

"Mom if you die, who has to pay the debts you still owe?"

With a slight smirk on my face I looked at my daughter and let her know, "If you want my belongings, you do!"

"That doesn't seem fair" my daughter replies. "The way I see it, if you die they should consider your debts paid!" What a concept! Unfortunately, that's not how it works. I continue by explaining to my daughter that I made a promise to pay back what I could not afford to pay at the original time of purchase, until the debt is paid in full. "It sure doesn't make sense to me to have someone else pay a debt that you owe," she says before walking away. Slowly turning and facing one another, we realize simultaneously the significance of the words she had just spoken.

Prepare yourself, because I am about to say something most would leave unsaid in the hopes of keeping you the reader. I find myself unable to keep quite because the "truth" is something we all have to face at some point in our lives. One of the main reasons people hate to hear the truth is that it hurts. Regardless of how you understand truth, I am about to share a truth with you that pertains to you, me, and every living being who has ever been or who will ever be. I don't care how much money you have, how much better off you think you are then your neighbor, how righteous you might think you are, how hard you think you work, or how beautiful you are, you've accumulated a debt that you alone could never repay—no matter how great your bank account is. Want proof? Well here it comes!

Adam and Eve were brought into a world that was made perfect by God. All God saw was perfection, but Satan with his less than desirable tactics sought to destroy that which God had made. From the moment Satan deceived Eve, sin found a way of insuring that the death of each and every one of us was immanent. Common sense tells each of us that we are eventually going to have to endure death. Some view death as the final chapter in a life that reached its full potential, in a life that sought refuge eating from a trash can with a card board box warming them at night, or the life of an individual who struggled under circumstances unbearable by most. The chapter may be over, but the book does not end there. Life does not end when the concrete slab sits snuggly over a vault that now contains the coffin where the individual now lies. As the dirt fills the hole that now contains what is left of the remains, the life of the individual will forever be changed according to the truths he or she chose to accept during his or her stay on this earth.

From the beginning of time, sin sought to destroy the souls of man. Satan devised a plan to deceive God's people, and he continues to deceive us today. Some believe money, popularity, and notoriety will be the building block for their eternal future. I fear not! The debt you and I have accumulated over time is sin. No plastic credit card with an unlimited amount of credit, no will leaving you an inheritance, no co-signer promising to pay your debts in the event you don't can pay the debt you and I owe for our sin. I'm a preacher, a follower of Christ, faithful to the church; you're not talking to me because I'm not a sinner. *Stop* deceiving yourself; we're all sinners! "For *all* have sinned and fall short of the glory of God." (Rom. 3:23 NIV)

I have to be truthful with you. Until each one of us recognizes the fact that no matter what stage of life we're in, what our financial status is, or what our public standing may be, when it comes to the end of our life, the *only* thing that will matter to God will be what the condition of our heart is. Believing that you have earned the right to enter into eternal life on your own accord is a serious miscalculation that you and I cannot afford to make. Your sin's and mine ensure us of one thing and one thing only—that is death. You and I cannot enter into the heavenly realms without understanding the magnitude of God's love for each of us.

Sin does not take God by surprise! I believe three of the most significant words God ever spoke were, "Let there be." With those three words, God spoke the foundation of the world into existence. In all His infinite wisdom, God knew that He was going to have to speak into existence a scapegoat to step in and make right what Satan sought to use for his own personal gain. Like a parent who vows to protect their children using all the means available to keep them safe, our Heavenly Father insured our safety by giving up a part of Him to save us all from eternal damnation.

God's measure of unconditional love caused Him to reach inside His very being and allow the unthinkable. Speaking through an angel to a willing vessel, God spoke into existence our kinsmen redeemer. From His very first breath of life, Jesus Christ became a threat to the very being whose sole purpose was to ensure each of us of one thing and that, my friend, was our demise! Satan himself sought the destruction of Jesus, making it his own personal conquest to ensure that He would fail. Traipsing around the countryside, Satan followed Jesus in an attempt to destroy the only hope you and I would ever have at redemption. God was well aware that His Son would have to endure the course laid out before Him. It is the unconditional love Our Heavenly Father has for each of us that He allowed this in an effort to save that which is lost, meaning you and I.

In a timely fashion, Jesus did exactly as His Father commanded Him to do. In the hours that preceded His death, Jesus in fear and in desperation, called out to His Father, saying, "Father, if Thou art willing, remove this cup from Me: yet not My will, but Thine be done." (Luke 22: 42 New American Standard) Enduring the false accusations by the very ones He came to save, enduring the humiliation of a mocked trial, and enduring the crucifixion upon the cross, Jesus Christ committed the most unselfish act ever known to man. I don't know if you can fully grasp the magnitude of what Jesus Christ did for you and me. See Jesus was perfect. He was sinless in all things. He did nothing that deserved death except love us beyond measure. Because of our sinful nature, God knew that He would have to send a substitute in our place to pay the ultimate price for a debt that we would accumulate and could never pay.

Comprehending the magnitude of God's love is something we may never fully do. But the one truth that we must accept is that it was God's unconditional love for us that paved the only way you and I could ever enter into our Heavenly inheritance. Our sin caused God to sentence His Son to death as a sacrifice for us all. It was the blood of Jesus Christ that was shed for you and I, that paid the price for our collection of debts (our sins), and that enabled us the only opportunity we would ever have at gaining entrance into Heaven.

Believing that God designed Heaven for the rich and famous, the bold and beautiful, or the faithful church attendee falls short of God's expectations of mankind. Weighing the debt of another's sin against your own is a manipulation tactic that may ease the mind but won't open a door closed by the Almighty God. Sin is sin and must be recognized as such no matter who commits it. Fame and fortune will not open the doors of Heaven for anyone; only the sincere belief that the blood of Jesus Christ was shed as a payment for the debts you and I accumulated, will.

My father is absolutely correct. As it stands the national debt will only increase and stands very little chance of ever reaching a zero balance in my lifetime or that of my children. We may never receive a "paid in full" statement for the debts that we have accumulated over time before our stay on earth is over. Death is immanent for each of us no matter what our religious affiliation, financial status, or our personal opinion of self may be. As you reach the final chapter in your life; your family and friends stand in bereavement recognizing your accomplishments; your coffin closed, sealed in a vault, covered with fresh earth, the question remains: where will you spend eternity?

My friend, there is nothing that you and I can do to pay off our debt of sin that we will continue to accumulate until the end of time. Our Heavenly Father sent His Son as a co-signer of sorts to pay a price for a debt we owe. My daughter's words, "It doesn't seem fair to have someone else pay for a debt you owe," stand true, but thank God, He saw it differently. It is my sincerest hope that by now no matter who you are, where you've come from, or where you're going you recognize your God loves you so much that He sent His only son to pay the ultimate price for our mistakes. Accept the gift that God has given you with a sincere heart, regardless of what anyone else thinks of you. God sent His Son to Calvary just so that you and I could share Heaven with Him.

"For the wages of sin is death, but the free gift of God is eternal life in Christ Jesus our Lord" (Rom. 6:23 New American Standard) Death is a promise. Jesus paved the only way for each of us to enter Heaven by taking our sins with Him and hanging on a cross as a payment for our debts. Don't let His death be in vain. Heaven is created for all those who have a humble heart and contrite spirit. God awaits and, my friend, it's not your bank account He is looking at; it's the condition of your heart that has His undivided attention!

Pray with me: Father, forgive me this day. Today, I want you to look at me and see the sinner that I am. I realize dwelling on what I have done or who I have become is of little importance. What is important to you, My Heavenly Father, is that I recognize how much you truly must love me because you allowed your Son to be led like a lamb to the slaughter for my sins.

Look at me alone, Lord. please understand that I am truly sorry and want to spend eternity with you. I fully comprehend how much you must love me because you sent your Son to die in my place. Thank you Father for you truly do love me unconditionally.

Your Sinner forever in your debt

_____ (your name)

Whosoever Will

In a world plagued with adversity, what chance does one stand in overcoming the odds in light of current circumstances? Watching the nightly news, one can assume that devastation somewhere in the world will be among the night's top stories. Job losses are at an all-time high, and the unemployment rate is expected to increase with the continuous decline in our current economy. Recession is rapidly becoming a word frequently used by economist around the globe, instilling fear in those who were once steadfast and strong. The war on terror is being fought abroad in an effort to detour further attacks on American soil; the inability to calculate the cost of the war is apparent as the lives of those lost are priceless from which ever side one chooses to view the spectrum. In these increasingly unsteady times, where exactly does one look for stability?

Throughout my studies, I've learned that it is God's desire for each of us to seek our own personal relationship with Him. God does not require a certain format with which one can achieve this relationship. "Come *as you are* before your God," is how I believe God perceives each of us. Compelled by this philosophy, I found myself recently alone with God deep in prayer, just Him and I. Raising concerns I had about the current state of our country, our economy, and the general direction we seemed to be heading in as a nation, I prayed, "Why are you just sitting by acting as though you are oblivious to what is happening all around us? Why, Lord, are you just watching us fall deeper and deeper into despair?" Believing that we should be up front and honest with God, I continued in prayer releasing it all to the One who knew exactly how I already felt. I continued praying, half angry at the way things were and the other half of me—if I am to be totally honest—irritated because I felt God was allowing all this happen, and He didn't care how worried or scared we were. I finished expressing my feelings to God and went to bed unsure that I had accomplished anything but felt better in spite of my uncertainties.

Under the cover of darkness, I found myself tossing and turning in and out of sleep, trying desperately to locate a comfortable position with which to find rest. In its place I found myself awoken by the very One who I had just hours before voiced my concerns to. Like a father who loves his child, Our Heavenly Father addressed the issue's I had brought before His throne. Clearly yet distinctively, God began, "Brenda, do you think that I am not aware of those things that are transpiring all around you?" He was making a statement in my opinion more than asking a question. "You warned them (a message I had preached to a body of believers months earlier) of My wrath being poured out on this nation. You told them that they must leave their wicked ways and seek My face as I had instructed." Without any hesitation our Heavenly Father proceeded by saying, "It is I who has poured out this wrath for my people have left their first love and have hardened their hearts toward me. I tell you though this very night that whosoever will call upon Me, I shall save, but know this night that My wrath has only just begun to be poured out." With that being said, I found myself no longer in His presence. Instead, all alone I was surrounded by complete darkness, and an unusual silence seemed to permeate the room.

As darkness turned into dawn, I found myself laying there, reeling from the words that had been spoken to me. A feeling of deep emptiness seemed to invade the spaces of my soul brought on by my fear for our nation or quite possibly the fear I felt when contemplating my own intentions. Reflecting over my own personal actions towards life's circumstances, I could see clearly how God had felt as though I had hardened my heart. I am well assured that my doubt about His willingness to help our nation and the tone I chose with which to address My Master only added to the negative feelings that stirred deep inside my being. God's message was clear, to the point, and spoke volumes!

Wrath is a word that should send shivers up and down our spines. Will you take a moment and reminisce with me? Do you remember what it was like when you were a child and you did something that met with your parent's disapproval? I don't mean something petty; I mean like maybe you saw something in a store that you just had to have. Perhaps you had no funds available with which to borrow from so you helped yourself to the item. You felt no guilt and no regrets as you walked home happy about what you presently had in your possession. Going home you found what you believed to be a secure place to hide your newly acquired item. Days turned into weeks and you had forgotten about that day all together. Life seemed to be going great, and then one day on the way home from school you had this unexplainable feeling churning inside your stomach. At first you ignored the feeling believing that it would soon pass, but you suddenly realized that it seemed to worsen with every step that took you closer to home.

Finally upon reaching your destination, you opened the front door happy at last to be home. Mom who usually greeted you on your arrival home from school was not at her usual post so you began going from room to room searching for the one person who could calm the stirring that seemed to have taken over your being. As you searched the house, you soon realized there was but one room left to check and that was your own. Slowly you opened the door and low and behold whose presence fills the room but your mother's and in her hand she stood holding the item you stole weeks earlier. The feelings that stirred inside of you moments earlier now seemed to dissipate as your mother stared at you with eyes that told a story of shame, hurt, and disappointment. Walking past you, clutching with both hands the item you couldn't do without, your mom left your room in silence, leaving you to ponder your actions and the consequences you've brought upon yourself. Time seemed to stand still as you played over and over again in your mind the wrath you must endure for the choice you made several weeks prior for an item you just could not live without and now wished you never had.

The above scenario pales in comparison when contemplating the wrath of God. I think that it bears mentioning that pondering wrath regardless of who will be the benefactor should make one conscientious of their own personal actions. Whatever your revelation of wrath may be, I think it's only fair to assume that God has warned us of His. In a distinctive voice our Heavenly Father said, "My wrath has only just begun to be poured out." I believe how each of us decides to interpret what God said will determine how surprised we are by his wrath.

The wrath of God is not a matter of if but when! I pose this question to each of you: with the credible warning of His impending wrath, will you be ready to suffer the consequences of your actions? Like the child who waits for his or her punishment for choices made, we to must face chastisement from the very One who created us.

And you have forgotten that word of encouragement that addresses you as sons:

My son, do not make light of the Lord's

Discipline,

And do not lose heart when he

Rebukes you,

Because the Lord disciplines those he

Loves

And he punishes everyone he accepts

As a son

(Heb. 12:5–6 NIV)

Rest assured that God is speaking to all of us no matter what our gender may be.

I can sugar coat this if I wanted to, but I am afraid making this sound like many of you would like to hear it would be contradictory to my objective. God's promise of wrath stems from our inability to live according to the guidelines set down before us by Him, either as individuals or as a whole. The perspective with which you choose to scrutinize the following is of course at your own discretion, but I find myself incapable of keeping to myself the truth that we must one day have to bear. As a nation, we have established that we are "One Nation under God," yet as individuals we stand in silence as we watch the liberty of our freedoms admonished by those who speak against the very God who created us. Perhaps we don't agree with those whose ideologies do not correspond with our own toward God, however, we let the voices of those who hold little regard for Him rise above our own, and in fact we embrace it and call it "change!"

I ask you, have we as a nation hardened our hearts toward God? We have allowed the removal of the Ten Commandments in public buildings, we have succumbed to public scrutiny on prayer in school, we are currently contemplating taking "One Nation Under God" from our pledge of allegiance, and "In God We Trust" has faced more opposition than the paper it's printed on. Is there any doubt about what would make God feel as though we've hardened our hearts toward Him? We have allowed the original foundation that was laid out before us by God to be manipulated, ridiculed, and removed. This demonstrates that we have become a nation that has no room for God in public places and show little regard for Him in our private lives! As I write this, I feel the tiny hairs on the back of my neck begin to stand. But we as a nation are indicating our need to continue to operate in rebellion against God, and His wrath is imminent due to the sincerity and our sheer determination to continue to act according to our rebellious nature.

Because I am involved with young people and try to keep their focus on God, I try hard to find anecdotes that concern Him. Recently, I read a passage about a little girl who was in search of a map of the United States; her sole desire was to learn where the states belonged on the map. Her father who was busy with his own concerns stopped what he was doing in an attempt to help his daughter with her relentless search. Finding a map in a magazine sitting on his desk, the little girl's father tore the map from its binder. In an attempt to occupy his daughter, the father ripped the map in several pieces before handing it to her. Using logic as a motive, the father told his daughter to go put the map back together and when she did, she would learn where the states belong. Leaving her dad with the puzzle in hand, the little girl busied herself with the task before her. Piece by piece the little girl put the ripped map back together. Taking it in her hands she went back to where she left her dad and showed him a map of the United States. Puzzled her father looks at her and said, "How did you do that so fast?"

"Simple," she told her dad, "On the reverse side of the map was a picture of Jesus Christ, and when I put Him back where He belonged, the United States just seemed to come together."

I think we can learn something from the wisdom that little girl discovered. Perhaps if we put God back to where He respectfully belongs, maybe things will once again come together for us as a nation. Weeks have turned into months now since God spoke to me, but I find myself in awe when I think of that night. Two words God spoke that night that seem to stand out were, "whosoever will." Those words indicate to me that God is open, willing, and ready, to establish a relationship with those willing enough to say, "Here I am!" The choice is yours of course, but the time is now! Procrastination only prolongs the inevitable. Like the child who faces a parent's wrath for a terrible miscalculation in judgment, we to must face the consequences of our actions.

The child in the previous scenario who stole from the store was none other than me. My purpose for sharing the memories of year's past stem from my desire to emphasize the fact that at times we all have had to surrender to the wrath of others for choices we made. However, I can honestly say that facing the wrath of my mother hurt little in comparison to the look of disappointment in her eyes. Many years have passed since that incident. Her disappointment faded, and it was her undying love for me that prevailed. God the Father spoke of His wrath and our nation that night. His disappointment in us is evident! But I do believe that in spite of our incredible errors in judgment, God's unconditional love for us will prevail. Perhaps we will never see the look of His disappointment that embellishes His face by our actions, but the sheer knowledge that comes from understanding that we are in fact hurting our Master should cause us to ponder our actions and perhaps change the direction our paths are heading. Thinking about the severity of God's words and His disappointment in us as a nation, I wonder why He would even bless us at all. I believe that if only one person surrendered to God's warning, He would bless, can you imagine how He would bless if we all did! The Father said "whosoever will," it's an open invitation won't you accept?

Different On Purpose

Let me express my deepest desire to achieve something worthwhile in this world before God initiates His plan into action and takes me home. My greatest accomplishment to date is the manner in which I have raised my daughters, assisting them in their endeavors to grow from the little girls they were into the young women they've become. I am presently in the midst of watching my son develop from the boy he is today into the man that he will become in the future. I have learned many lessons through out my experiences of motherhood but none as significant as the ones taught by those whose little fingers fit perfectly when intertwined with mine and whose eyes share a similar resemblance.

Are you aware of the fact that there are considerable differences between siblings? Although my oldest daughter and my youngest daughter are close in age, they share very few similarities. On the contrary, my son and youngest daughter who have a considerable age difference between them are similar in many ways. In fact, there are times when my son does something that my youngest daughter used to do, and I just sit there and say to myself, "Didn't this already happen to me once before?" In an effort to rationalize my children's differences, I must first accept them as individuals and recognize they are diverse from one another in spite of their likenesses. No matter what effort I put forth as a parent to try to create similarities between my three children, they were created to look and act differently. Nothing can change that factor and nothing is supposed to.

Have you ever had someone approach you and say, "Are you sure you don't have a twin?"

You come back and say, "No, when they made me they broke the mold." Although a cliché, that statement holds some deep sentiments. Perhaps you may have features that bear a resemblance to someone or a disposition that resembles a similar likeness to another. Nevertheless, in spite of certain similarities, you are uniquely different. In fact, each of us was outfitted by our Heavenly Father with our own set of defining characteristics that He exclusively designed to coincide with our personality that now make up our being.

Here is where I hope to reach out and achieve my intended goal from the beginning of the book. My purpose for writing this text was not to establish the fact that I can mix words or facilitate proper grammar in context. My sole intention has been to touch someone who was looking for a reason to face another day or perhaps just needed someone to tell him or her that life in all its complexities is worth living. Excuse me for being candid with you, but I feel as though there are some of you reading this that doubt your significance, your worthiness, and believe whole heartedly that you are of little value to yourself or anyone else for that matter. I am going to put forth every effort in an attempt to change your personal perspective.

Perhaps you are wondering why I pointed out the fact that there are major differences between my three children at the beginning of this chapter. I wanted you to understand that although they may be from the same bloodline, they are different on purpose. When God created my children, He formed them, breathed on them, and then gave them life, setting them apart from one another with a specific focus in mind. Regardless of my expectations of my children, it was God's initial plan that was to be forthcoming; I was just an instrument that He used to bring into being His plan for their lives.

What does that have to do with you? Just like when forming my children, God looked to and fro before He made you and thought that the world needed something more. After careful consideration, God saw that His world although perfect seemed to be lacking something of significant importance. So God began molding clay with His two hands, transforming it into a relic that was far beyond extraordinary. The piece that captivated God's undivided attention was molded differently from any other that He had crafted before. As God finished perfecting that which was before Him, He set His creation down, examined it, and saw that it was good. My friend the finished product that fascinated the Creator Himself was not just a mere piece of pottery but a beautiful vessel unlike any other. The vessel that the Maker just could not visualize His world being without was you! Hand crafted by the Master Potter was a perfected vessel, brought to life, to be different on purpose from all the other vessels, to be used as an instrument in Gods perfect plan.

I hope that I have succeeded in my attempt to convince you of how important you and I are to the Creator. In fact God could not see His world perfected without you and me in it. Perhaps the world may not accept who we are, but God accepts us as we are! What I am trying to convey to you is that regardless of circumstance, our existence was not just a mere coincidence or an accident that just happened. The Creator Himself specifically took His time in developing the being that you and I are today. Try as we may to dispute the significance of our existence or worth only insults the intelligence of the Almighty God. I would suggest that now is as good a time as any to stop allowing Satan to deceive you and to accept that although different by comparison you are exactly as God intended.

I cannot express to you how important our existence is to God and how relevant it may be to mankind. Doubting our purpose for existing may be a ploy from the enemy in an attempt to curtail that which God had intended for us from the very beginning of our life. Contrary to what we may want to believe, our existence was and is a part of God's plan. However, I am compelled to tell you that it is not above Satan to disrupt God's plan. In fact, if I were to be totally honest with you, it is Satan's earnest desire to keep God from enacting His plan into action in our lives.

We must not allow Satan to divert our focus, or he will delay our ability to carry out our intended purpose implemented by the Creator Himself. My dear friend, time is of the essence. We cannot afford any more delays. Satan would love nothing better than for us to believe that our life is not worth living, that we have no direction with which to live our life, and that our very existence serves no purpose. Excuse me, but he is dead wrong! If by chance you are currently entertaining those thoughts, it's high time for you to tell Satan to back off. For it was God Himself that formed you and me long before our mothers even knew anything about us. He did so with a specific purpose in mind and our very existence is as crucial today as it was all those years ago when He saw that the world needed something more and brought our existence into being.

God is counting on each of us to implement His plan into action, but we cannot do that if we continue to allow Satan to restrain us. From the start of this book, my intentions have been to see those who deem themselves unworthy to rise up and recognize God's gift of compassion for those with whom He created. I cannot reiterate enough the love God the Father has for you and me in spite of who we may be or what we may have become. For that reason, now is the time, my friend that you get up from where you've been, stop looking back, and move in a forward motion toward the mercy and grace that Jesus Christ gave His life for on the cross. Until we make the initial decision to see past where we've been, we will never get to where we are supposed to be. Therefore thwarting the purpose for which you and I were initially created.

My dear friend, God in all His infinite wisdom knew what His intentions were for you and me from the beginning of time. Although we may be different by comparison, God needs each and every one of us just the way we are. If you're under the impression that God is only seeking out the perfect people to enact His plan, you are sadly mistaken! There was only One who was perfect, and He gave His life so you and I could live ours. Perfection was met many years ago on a hill called Golgotha, a hill that claimed the life of Jesus Christ, our Savior who gave His life in our place, "paying a debt He didn't owe, for a debt we couldn't pay."

God sent His Son to die in our place. Doubting our ability to be useful or doubting our worth only proceeds to diminish the significance of what God did for us. I don't know where you are in life, but right now I want to speak not to your mind but to your heart. Before you read any further, please ask God for understanding and ask Him to open your heart so that you may fully comprehend what He wants you to grasp from the following. Heavenly Father bless the heart of your chosen ones, as they read the following. Oh, God, only you know what you want them to receive from it. Reach into the depths of their soul, oh God, I pray for understanding in Jesus name.

The worth of a person is not weighed by his or her prosperity but by what resides deep within the confines of his or her soul! Man measures worth by looking at the success of the individual.

God measures worth by looking merely at the individual. Living to impress the multitudes defines the character of a self-made man; living to impress the Master defines the character of a man whose soul is worthy. Man will put you on a pedestal and remove you just as quickly. God calls you His chosen regardless of status. Man will turn a blind eye to the less fortunate; God calls them His beloved. Man looks upon the world and passes judgment; God looks upon the world and judges man. The worth of a man is not what is apparent to the world but what lies hid beneath the surface that can only be seen by God Himself. I ask you, my friend, if God chose today to look deep within your soul, what exactly would He see?

It is not my intention to judge the soul of a man but to acknowledge the fact that the worth of a man is not what he possesses but what he professes. The man who seeks shelter under a cardboard box and praises God for His generosity will gain so much more than the man who has much and praises himself for his success. Again my intention is not to downplay the significance of one's success or the lack there of but to establish the fact that it's not how successful the individual is but to whom the individual credits his or her success. What is of extreme importance is the fact that you recognize it's not what you have in this life that defines your character but who you become in light of it.

Different on purpose is how God designed each of us. Doubting our worth diminishes the significance of what the Master Potter did all those years ago when He realized His world was

incomplete without you and me. In spite of your current circumstances have you ever wondered what God's purpose was for
creating you? Have you ever stopped dwelling on yourself long
enough to ask God what your purpose for existing is? My friend,
you will never know what your intended purpose in this life is
until you ask your Heavenly Father. Only God knows what His
plans for you are. All I can do is assure you that if by chance you
believe you have no purpose, you're wrong about yourself because
God never made anything He didn't deem necessary, worthy, or
useable. Time is short, my friend. Accept your uniqueness as a gift
from God, thank Him, and ask Him what it is He needs you to
do to make His world a better place.

Before I Go

I am about to conclude this book, but before I go I want to share some personal thoughts with you. I want you to imagine God sitting up on the throne in front of a big desk, busy with the works of creating His world and perfecting it according to His plan. After being busy for six days, God takes off His glasses and reclines back in His chair to enjoy some much-needed rest. As a new day dawns, God finds Himself well rested. He leans forward and begins to prepare for the day ahead. As He prepares for the day, He searches for the glasses He had so diligently laid down the day before. Relentlessly searching for His missing glasses, God glances over His desk and looks down upon His creation. It is then that God realizes that it was not He that misplaced them.

During God's well deserved rest, the world came by His desk and helped themselves to His glasses. As the world put on God's glasses, people began taking matters into their own hands, judging the world one individual at a time as though they were He. My friend, it is imperative that you understand what I am trying to convey to you. The world is made up of people who have made it their prerogative to persistently pick up God's glasses and pass judgment upon you. I am here to inform you that the way the world sees you, views you, or perceives you is not in the same manner that your Heavenly Father looks at you. The world may have picked up God's glasses and put them on, but the world is still looking at you through their own eyes and not His!

In truth each of us could be found guilty of picking up God's glasses and passing judgment. On numerous occasions, I have taken it upon myself to decide the fate of another, only to realize later in my alone time with God that I am no different in the eyes of God the Father than those whom I have passed judgment upon. In my own personal conquest to please God, I was in fact hurting the very ones He looked upon and called beloved. What each of us needs to fully understand is that in our attempt to judge who is right and wrong, we have proceeded to place ourselves in God's position, presenting ourselves as being His equal. When God looked to and fro and thought that the world needed something more, He created each of us with a specific purpose in mind, but you and I can rest assured it was not His intention that we take His place. We were created to assist God in His endeavor to save those who are lost, and we cannot do that by looking through God's glasses and judging the world accordingly.

Please understand that it is not my intention to portray God with glasses. My sole intention is to bring to light that we may in fact judge others as though we are looking at them through God's eyes. Only when we realize the error of our ways will we stop fulfilling our own fleshly desires and begin to fulfill God's intended purpose for our lives. We are different on purpose, but in the eyes of God the Father we are exactly what He intended from the beginning of time. If we would take off God's glasses and just see people for what they are and accept them as they are, perhaps then God would be able to reveal His intended purpose for our lives and theirs as well. Those whom we pass judgment upon could quite possibly be a miracle in the making.

Before I leave you, I have something I want you to reflect upon from this day forward. God the Father is *Soul'D Out* in love with you. If by chance you are still in doubt, take some personal time right now and talk one-on-one with Him. Perhaps you've never talked to Him, maybe you don't know how to talk to Him, or you feel you've made a mess with your life and He doesn't want to talk to you. The God I serve is looking down from the throne room of Heaven in all His majesty and glory thinking to Himself, "My poor child, if only you knew how much I truly love you. In fact, I love you so much that I sent My only Son to wipe away the sins of the world and that, my beloved child, includes yours. I have loved you unconditionally even when you made your bed in hell. I was there with you every step of the way, and I am here with you today as you sit and wonder why I would even care. My precious child, I will forgive you for all you've done. All you have to do is ask Me. It is my greatest intention that you be with me once I call you home. I can make you choose Me, but I won't. I want you to love Me as much as I love you, but only at your choosing. Please don't wait, for I have not promised you tomorrow and today could be your last. I love you. Here I am my beloved child. I eagerly await our visit. Do not fear Me for I have waited for this day for so long.

I leave you with this: A man died and went to heaven. As he went past the pearly gates, the man was greeted by Saint Peter who was assigned the task of giving him the grand tour of his new home. As they strolled down the streets of gold, they passed a building open on both ends, and the man noticed that Saint Peter walked on by without taking him inside. Questioning Saint Peter, the man asked, "What is in there?"

Saint Peter quickly responded, "Nothing, you don't want to go in there!" In spite of the beauty that surrounded the man, he just couldn't erase the thought of that building from his mind.

So again he questioned Saint Peter, "What's in that building back there?"

Again Saint Peter responded, "Nothing, you don't want to go in there!"

Finishing their tour of heaven, they returned back to the pearly gates, and again the man saw the building. However, this time the man didn't ask Saint Peter instead he impatiently said, "I want to go in there!"

Saint Peter then told him, "Okay but I am telling you, you really don't want to!" Running inside the building, the man saw boxes on top of boxes, each of them engraved with a name.

Questioning Saint Peter he asked, "Is there one in here with my name on it?" Saint Peter simply pointed to a single box with his name engraved on it.

Excited about what could possibly be inside the box the man slowly began to open it, but again Saint Peter warned, "I am telling you that you really don't want to open that!" The man ignoring the warning of Saint Peter opened the box before him. As the man opened the box, tears of despair began to roll down his face. Closing the box and turning away the man began sobbing uncontrollably.

Saint Peter looked at the man heart broken and said, "Now you see why I didn't want you to see what was in there!" The man picked up the box and put it back where he had found it, and as he walked out of the building, he turned around one last time looking at all the boxes with names written upon them.

The saddened man then thought to himself, "If only I could tell them!"

My dear friend, what could have possibly been in the box that caused the man so much pain in the most elegant place in the universe? My desire is not to leave you in suspense, but to make you wonder why a man who left this life and entered into eternity could possibly be saddened by anything within its confines. It is not God's intention for us to cry when we get to heaven, but I wonder if the tears that the man endured were in fact self-inflicted.

The box engraved with the man's name placed inside a building within the Heavenly realms was placed there for God's personal use. My friend, that box was God's way of storing the blessings He wanted to pass on to the man while he was here living on earth. What the man saw when he opened up his box, were all the blessings God had every intention of giving to him, but the man while living on earth never opened himself up to receive them. Therefore, when the man opened up the box he saw all that God had intended to give him, but never did because he never afforded the Master the opportunity.

When this life is over, and it will eventually end, the choices we have made while living here on earth may in fact cause us to cringe once we reach our eternal destination. I want you to consider your walk in life up to this point. Along the journey, could you have possibly missed out on opportunities to receive from the Master blessings that you were never willing to accept?

What happened yesterday is gone. What happens in our future is up to each of us. Our boxes are full, and the Creator awaits. It is His intention to bless us, but it's up to each of us to look inside our own soul to see what could possibly be obstructing the hand of God from moving in our life. Only I can stop God from blessing me, and only you can hinder God's attempt to give to you what He desires you to have.

About The Author

Brenda L. Boyd is the mother of three, and the daughter and sister to a large yet very close family. Her desire in life is to reach out to all those who deem themselves unworthy of Gods loving mercy, and she yearns for the day when these individuals discover the grace that only God the Father can give through His unconditional love for each of us. She longs to spend eternity within the confines of the heavenly realms but understands that life's obstacles stand between herself and them. Realizing that this world is made up of those whom God calls His beloved children, she keeps her focus centered on building up His kingdom one soul at a time, in spite of whom they are or who they may have become.

LaVergne, TN USA
01 November 2009

162614LV00004B/5/P

9 781449 033569